Scribbles & Coddles

The Illustrated Poetry of Bob Komives

Scribbles & Coddles

The Illustrated Poetry of Bob Komives

Third Edition

ISBN: 978-1-7338841-4-3

Published in the United States of America, 2021, by RPK Press, Fort Collins.

(1st Edition published, 2018)

Cover design: Becky Hawley Design

RPK Press
324 East Plum Street
Fort Collins, CO 80524

If I were not afraid to be the fool
I would play openly with children's toys,
drink cheap scotch from time to time,
eat fried Spam out of nostalgia,
wear white socks and loafers.

I would not twice-check my zipper.
I would not worry that you laugh at me,
because I enjoy helping you laugh.
I imagine I could even speak of sport in symphony hall,
and, in Lisbon, call forth my few words of Portuguese.
I would be unafraid to praise our enemy
—criticize our friend.
I would admit I still love you.

If I were not afraid to be the fool
I would dance when I feel dance,
and,
as I always do,
I would sing off-key,
—but loudly again as unharnessed child.
If I were not afraid to be the fool,
indeed, I would be less foolish.

Bob Komives, 2021

as the road is to follow

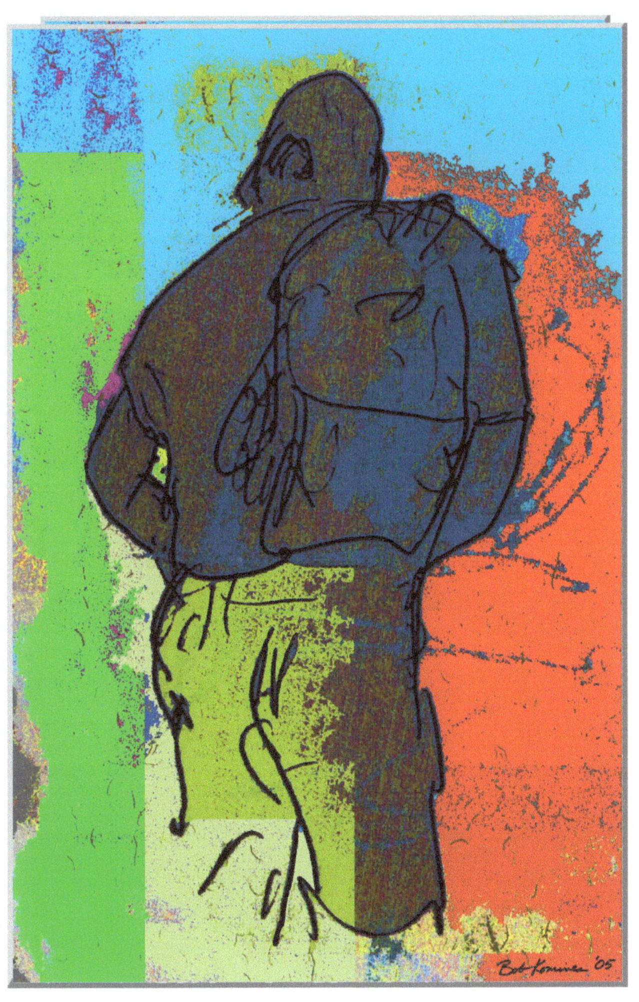

On The Art Of Synthesis

I found a faint road through a vast field
where genius, fool, and charlatan must ply.
As hard as the road is to follow,
harder still is to know who am I.

Yes, Yes I Was

Back then,
I was the only person in the world
who wore flip-flops
off the beach
and
out of the shower.
Yes I was.
Yes, yes I was.
My loved ones (embarrassed)
wanted me in Birkenstocks.
Yes they did.
Yes, yes they did.

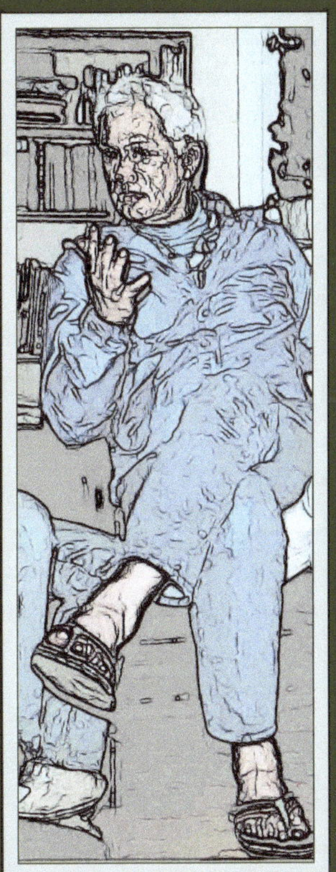

Scribbles & Coddles

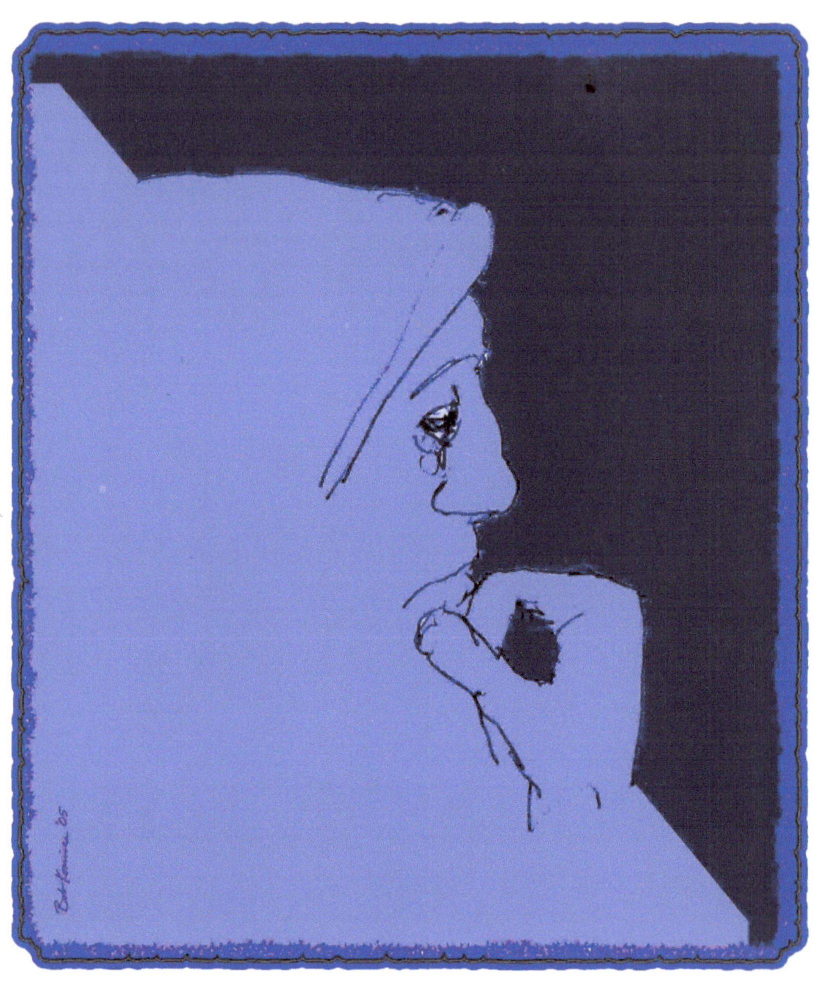

I plan to scribble this week:

both a picture and a poem.

Read this week:
something neglected
and sitting around.

Study this week:
language and science,
new and forgotten.

I plan:
to prune and weed—a little,
coddle a fresh egg and some older scribbles,
cobble a little table,
do a little healthful exercise.

This week will likely:
surprise me
at unplanned time
with something and someone new,
take me
over sad-but-noble miles
to new ashes of old friend,
give me
a moment or two
for these thoughts
and thoughts of you.

After A Long Pause

As often happens, someone asked

how he became so successful. He smiled:

I owe it to advice I got from my uncle as I boarded the ship to leave the old country.

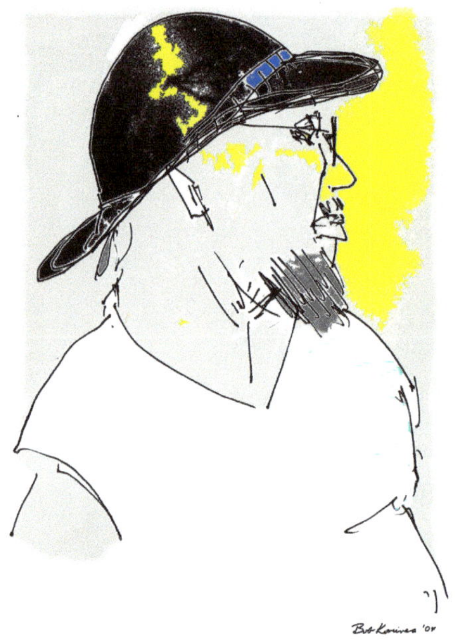

Never say never nor always;
people can always prove you wrong.
Seldom say sometimes or maybe;
people may at times find you timid.
Be moderate in all things,

lest you grow old too quickly.
Yet, never be excessive in your moderation,
lest you forget what it is to be young.
On Tuesday and Thursday
be sure to look before you leap.
Other days,
do not be he who hesitates.
Know that he who has no rules is yet to be born;
he who has no exceptions has yet to live.
Take ownership of your future
or of your past
never of both.
Finally,
repeat good advice by the whole
and live the best advice by halves.

As often happens,
after a long pause,
someone asked his opinion of the weather.

Deep Embrace

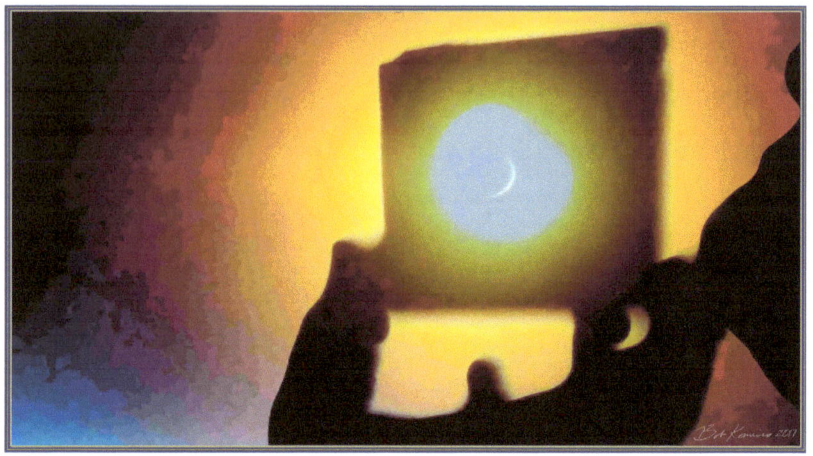

Times change;
Earth and Heaven move
when,
in the marrow of one breastbone,
steep ego
and
deep humility
embrace.

More Truthful Confession

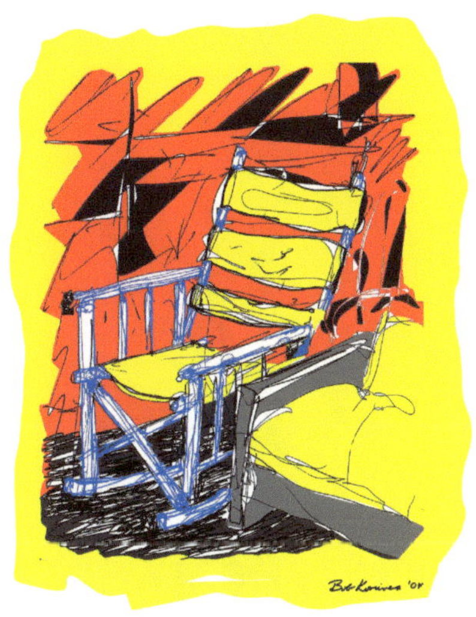

Ah, Genius of Science,
I confess I owe you much
for chasing off my curable ignorance
and my primitive superstitions.
Yet,
here lingers
  an armchair romance,
    a well-couched prejudice,
      a naive daydream,
        a more truthful confession:
A favorite few came back.

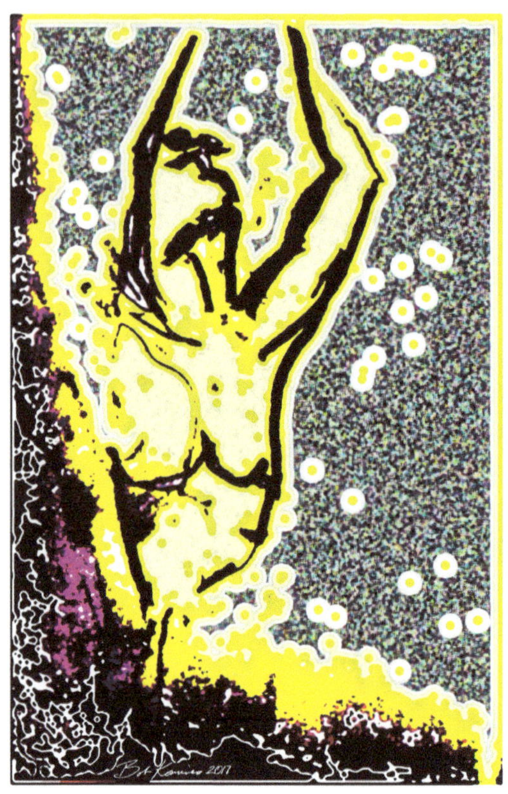

From branch quite alive
this beautiful leaf falls to its death
to be reborn as nourishment
for same branch,
old tree, new leaf.

Life is rough
and life is good.
Land is rough,
but land is good.

Waters get rough
and harm us,
yet water is good;
it enlivens us.
Our past taught hard lessons
as it brought all that is good.

From branch quite alive
this beautiful leaf falls to its death
to be reborn as nourishment
for same branch,
old tree, new leaf.

Light and Shaded Errands

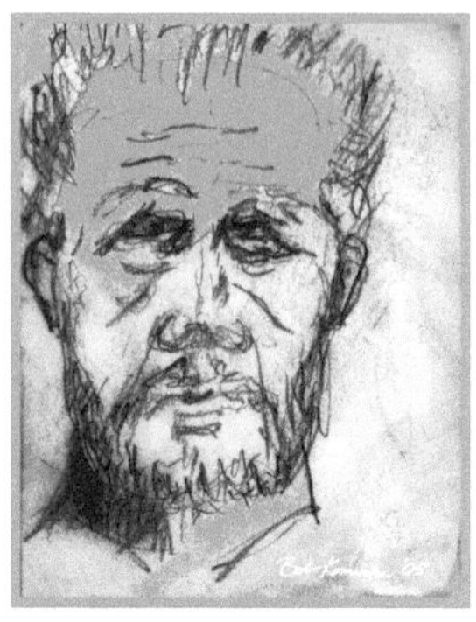

I remember how pleasurable it once felt
to work all day in the heat
and, at day's end,
feel a satisfied weariness,
those soothingly-sore muscles,
my self-righteous thirst.
Today,
it took but an hour to get there
and, once there,
to search for that lost pleasure
and those hidden adjectives.
Ah, but tomorrow all day
I shall find pleasure
in light and shaded errands.

Not About Perfections

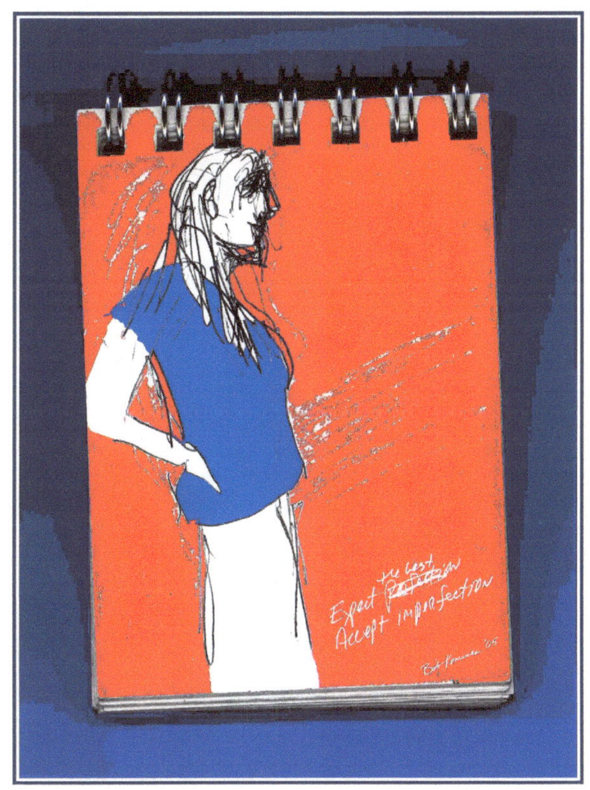

'not about perfections,
nor to be better,
nor to better it;
but about adventure,
for the great heavens
and the hell of it.

The Close Guilt

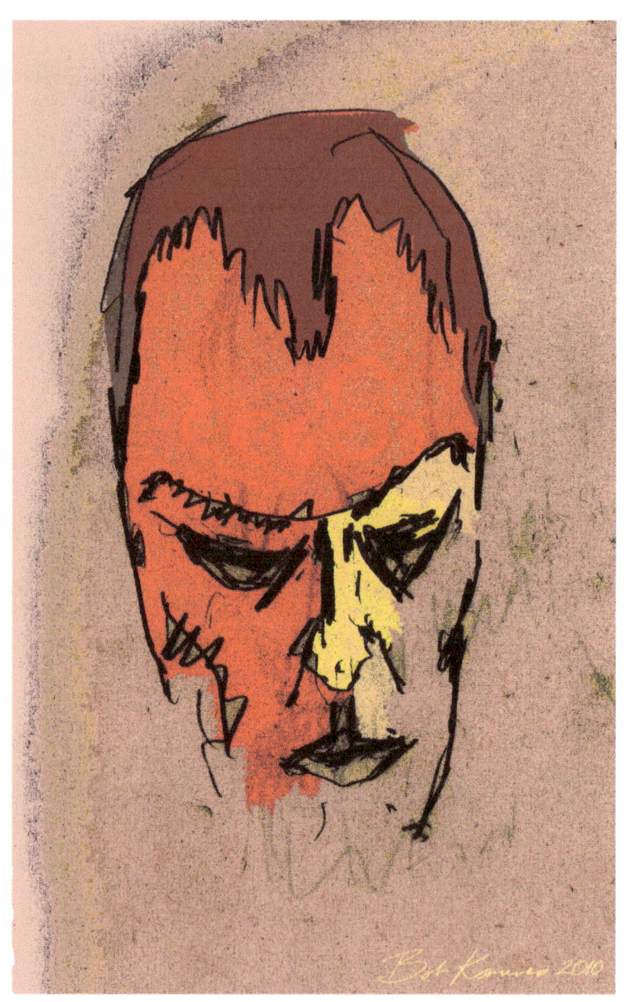

Who bears the close guilt
for friendship severed
by distant attack on Fort Sumter?

Noon Dawn

They may remember
a too-long year
365 days
nineteen more
twelve more hours
until noon dawn
of too-long sought year
ours
drawn two weeks
too weak
to strength
Kristalltag to *Schönertag*
mourning through morning
until sun of everyone
rose again
at noon.

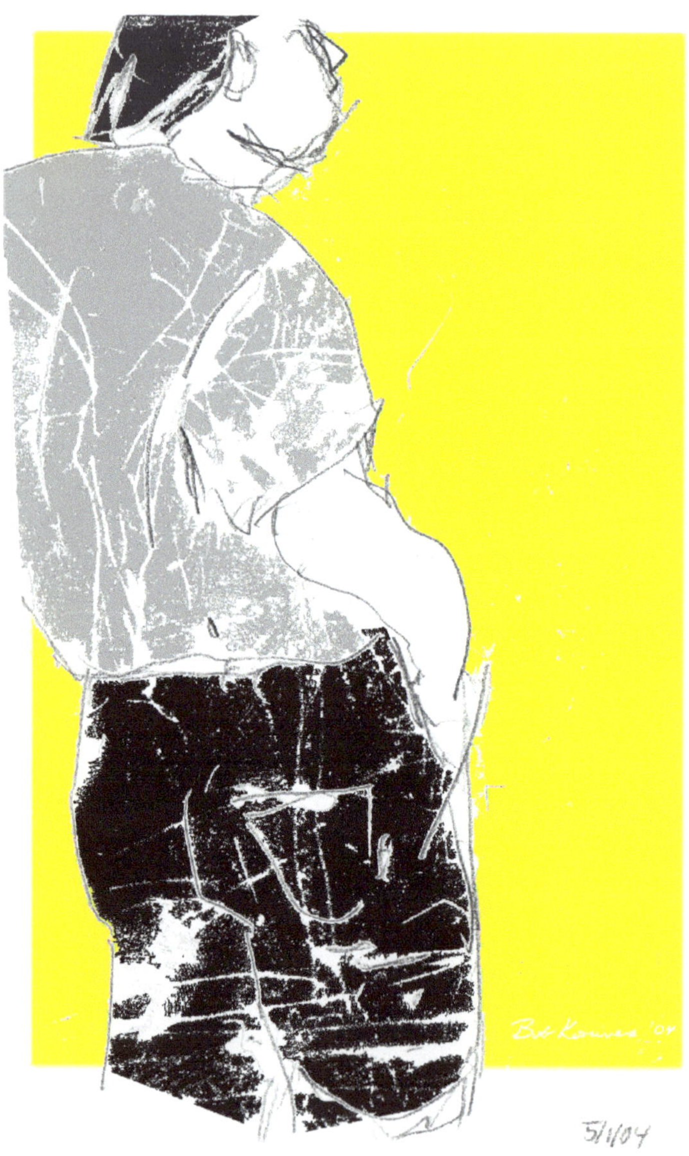
5/1/04

Ganas

Yesterday's easy task,
—a bother to do—
—important to do—
remains undone.
Yesterday's task,
—yet more difficult today—
—yet more important tomorrow—

Dismay.
Task has grown.
I have withered.

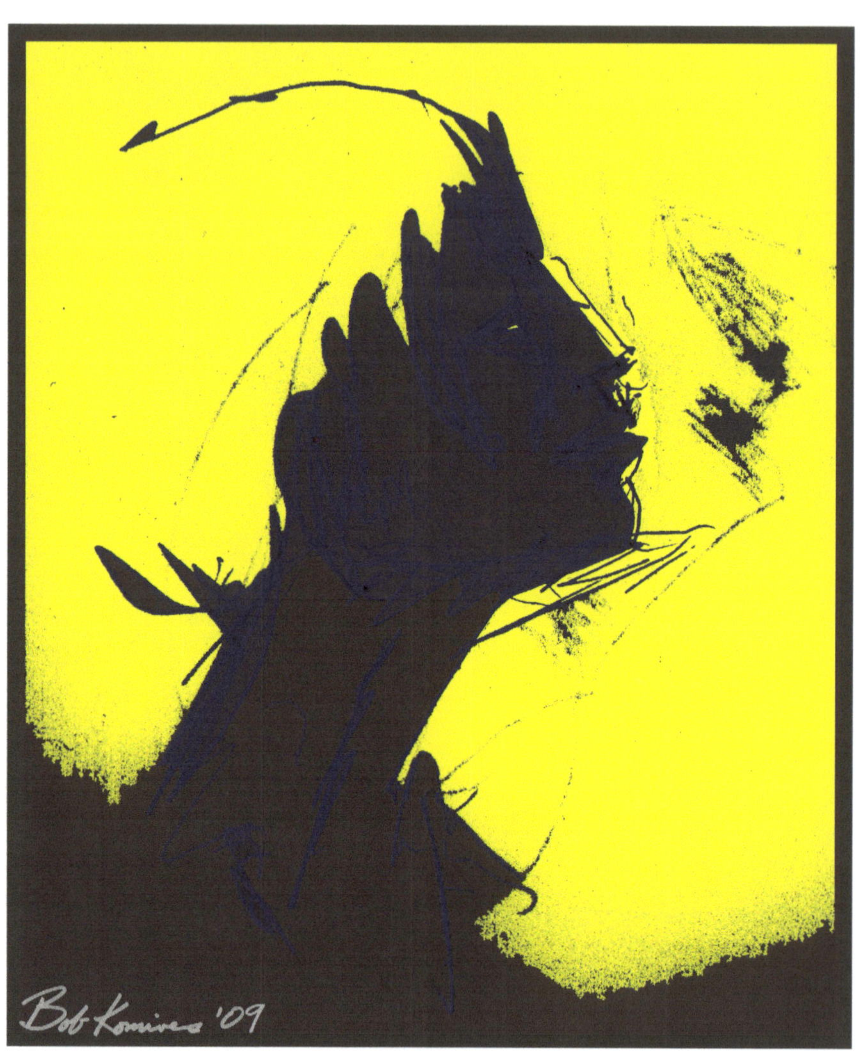
Bob Komives '09

Must and Will

As a planet knows its sun and spin,
I must know my self.
As a river is its bed and flow,
I must be myself.

As each moment fills and embraces its space,
I must embrace and love me.

Now,
(while I work my way there)
As a fawn enjoys its wobble,
I will let me.

I Say

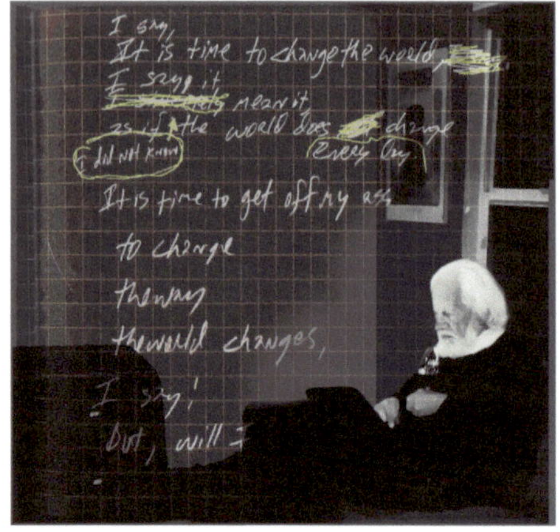

I say,

it is time to change the world,

I say it,

mean it,

as if I did not know

the world does every day change.

It is time to get off my ass

to change

the way

the world changes.

I say!

But, will I?

Renovation

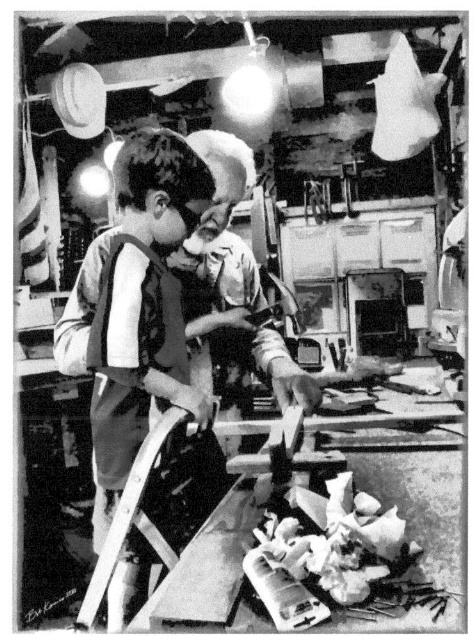

Hammer
pound
ten-penny nail.
Board
cut
paint
pail.

Pipe
fitting
duct
tape.
Dust
plaster
undo
make.

Muscle
finesse
precision
eye.
Lift
pull
screw
pry.

Order
mess
disorder
clean.
Count
draw
stand
lean.

Nuts
bits
apron
gloves.
Callous
cuts
nudge
shove.

End today
tomorrow again.
Crosscut
rip
break
mend.

Strip wire
wind tight.
Black to black,
white to white.

Climb ladder
two-by-four.
Crowbar
pencil
chisel
door.

Hangers
drivers
inches
pound.
Levels
bevels
squares
round.

Eight-penny
too many
too short
too long.
Measure twice
remember wrong.

Joist
hoist
tacky
dry.
Smooth
moist
give-up
try.

To frame
and sheathe
to trim
and bend.
Length
to width
to end again.

Hole or Castle

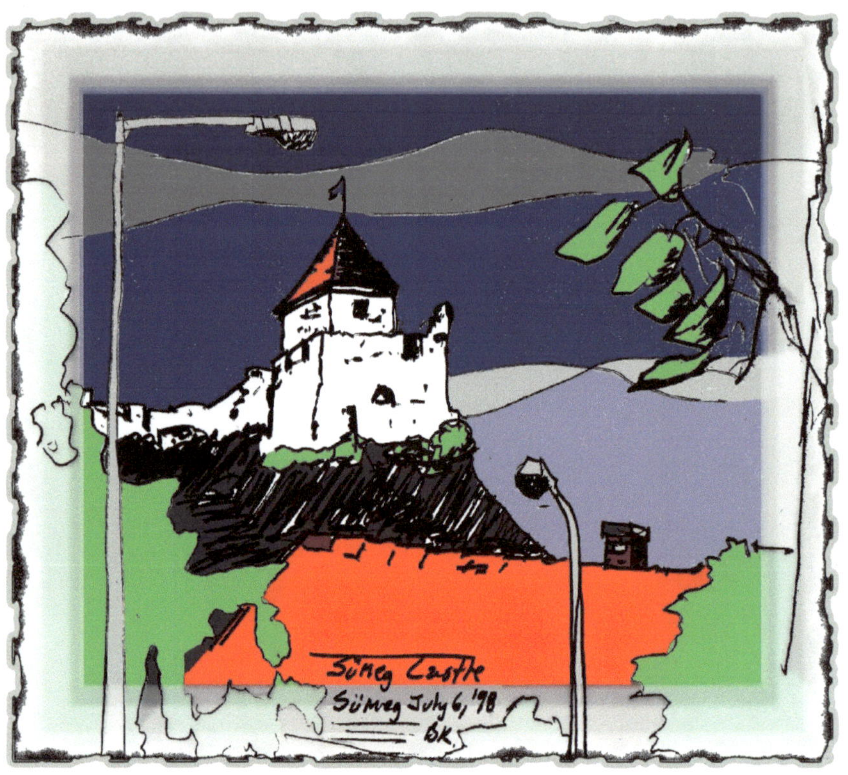

To hide

or to defend yourself

from the marauding horde,

will you build a high-fortress-castle,

or will you dig a low-hole?

Castle seems more pleasant
—more generous with status.
(Compare castled duke with lowly caveman)

Castle gives an image of protection.
(impregnable to all but the pregnator)

Hole, perhaps, is less the target.
The proud marauder,
looking up,
may miss your hiding place,
or see no glory in it,
or show you mercy if you point to a castle.

As for me:
in peace, I still love to play in castles;
in crisis, I may have to seek a hole;
but don't ask me to build or dig.
Let me, instead, wander the land
learning paths that cross frontiers.
For, with the luck of rumor or warning,
I will prefer to walk away.

Music, No Dance

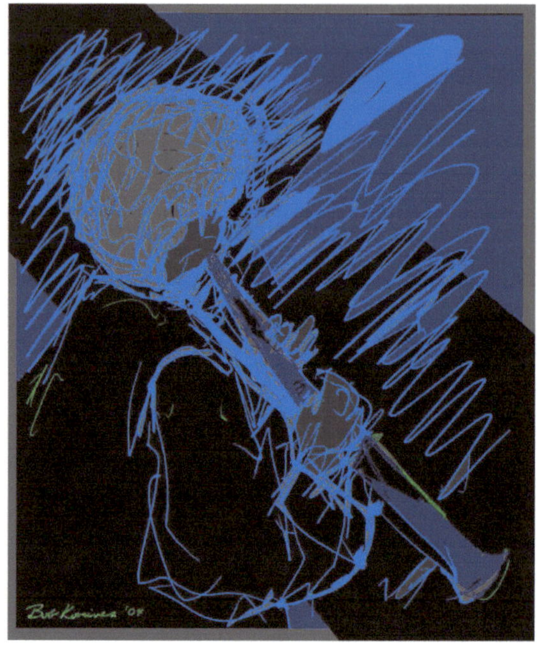

Music, no dance.

Yawn, no weary.

Middle of town.

Middle of nowhere.

Last boom is gone.

Next boom is waiting.

Old bodies have gone.

New ghosts keep coming.

Too few to be danced.

Too dead to be weary.

In Each of My Prisons

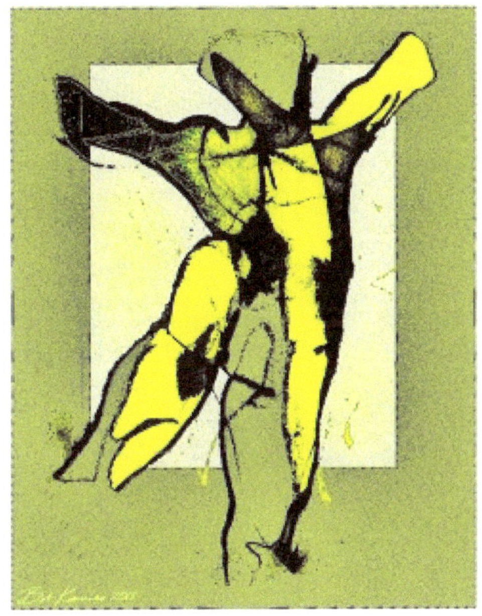

Free me, and I find my limits;
enslave me, and I find yours.

In each of my prisons, a freedom;
within each freedom, a prison;
released by the other to be held in by another
to trouble
with struggles
that double
as my liberation.

Thoughts on Coming Back and Going Back

Do choose well your timing.

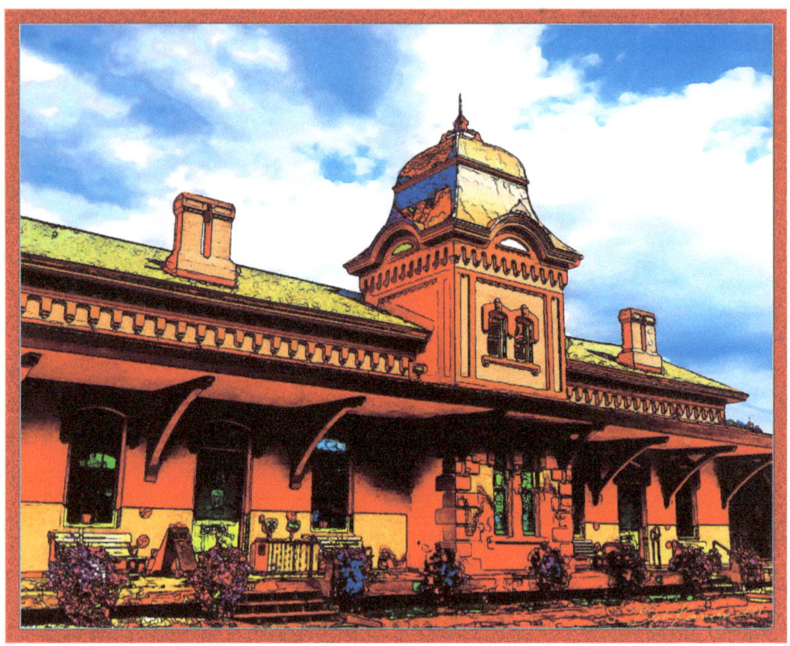

We made no mistake to promise a better future,
at least, no mistake, to set such hope.
We did mistake to blame the past,
to forget that past is not by blame undone.
It comes back in anger to ambush:
    the promise not realized,
    blemish not obscured,
    war not ended,

life, in death not replaced,
design, in imitation perverted,
adventure paused,
experiment not perfected,
success not humbly accepted.

His year ended in September,
headed back out on an airplane:
through suspended time
to apprentice languages
and still new countries.

She found herself among the regulars,
sipped her beer,
wrote and watched,
listened to their strange words:
wishing to be of them,
pleased to be outside
looking in,
taking notes,
the audience alone,
drama and comedy,
back and forth,
a rush,
a calm,

floors swept,
regular customers
back for their usual,
out and gone forever.

Tomorrow,
fly off to your new life in the Americas:
the lands of hope and prosperity
where you have lived fifty years.

Harvest the welcomes and rejections.
Start anew.

You were back three days
before the familiar knock
came back through your conscience wall:
what will you do?
how will you earn?
when will you answer?
and in answering
(just to answer)
what will you by default decide?

What will we be next year?
How long will we be?

If she writes poetry for a third year
has she come back a poet?
If he finishes his family's spoken history
has he returned an historian?

You help family and friend
if you come back with a better label:
        for yourself, a better label.

Coming back or going back,
what we call you
is what we believe of you
in the little time we have to think of you.

I come back to what is familiar:
        to skies
        bluer than I can recall,
        to arms and smiles
        more than I knew,
        to smells
        I remember only when I walk into them.

He came back because this is home:
        the place he comes back to.
He came back here
because he had gone back there:

as a visitor returning into history,
to the rugged works
of people seven hundred years older,
to the strange language
each time less strange,
to greetings by more friends than remembered,
to towns
more like home than expected,
at home
yet away from home
in a place that home will never be.

You have come from one hundred places
and have gone back to fifty.
In thirty you felt things familiar
that somehow welcomed you.
In twenty-nine the welcoming expectations are few,
and the mystery is great.
In one the expectations are many;
the mystery is thought to be gone.

As visitor,
you were at home in simple familiarity.

Here, in familiar complexity,

you are near-native.

Homes away from home:
    freedom and wonder,
    at worst, dissipation.

Home, itself, is a cave,
if on a great flat plain,
if in a sunlit treetop:
    comfortable and enveloping,
    a base and a discipline,
    at worst, confinement.

"Coming and going"
    (you might say)
"are just a matter of timing."
Timed poorly,
you may bounce
    between confinement and dissipation.
Timed well,
you can float
    between discipline and freedom.

In coming back and going back,
do choose well your timing.

To Know How to Wonder

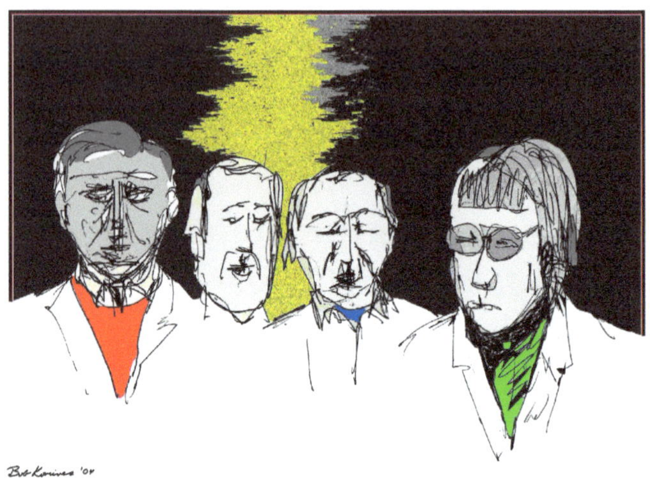

We know.

We know we know the answers.

What to do.

How.

And why.

We know we know.

The false.

The true.

The tried.

Few

    are the questions,

and fewer

    the answers we cannot grasp.

And at these few
    we know to wonder.
Indeed, this is life gifted full:
    to know what we know,
    yet know how to wonder.
Yet, fuller still in our discovery:
    they know,
    and they wonder too.
We
    and they.
Know
    and wonder.
Path to peace!
    To human perfection?
No.
This path remains our dream.
And we must know that we know why.
And we must permit ourselves to wonder
    how future binds to history.
Today, again:
    at which we wonder, they know;
    at which we know, they wonder.

kind of love

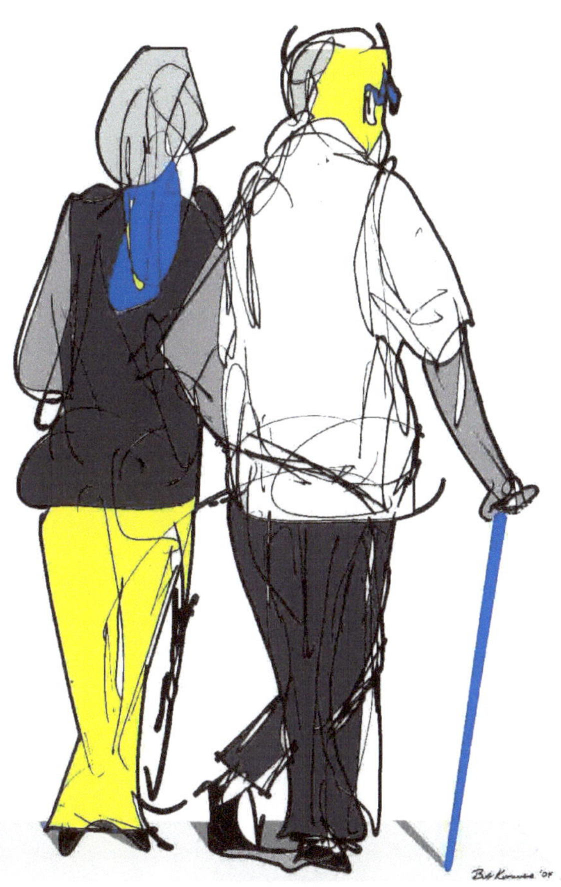

If There Were but One Kind of Love

If there were but one kind of love
we are lovers;
we are friends.
In turns, we would be
parent,
child,
favored neighbor,
distant kin.
You would find me as cuddly as your favorite book
—a book that we would neither buy nor sell,
  for that would be slavery.

Knowing but one kind of love
you would understand my caress of a beautiful dance;
find me jealous of your banana split,
offer equal gifts to beloved sunrise and favorite uncle.
bestow like kiss upon kitten, tulip, and lip.

If there were but one kind of love
I would feel as much nostalgia for this moment
—too beautiful and fresh to forget—

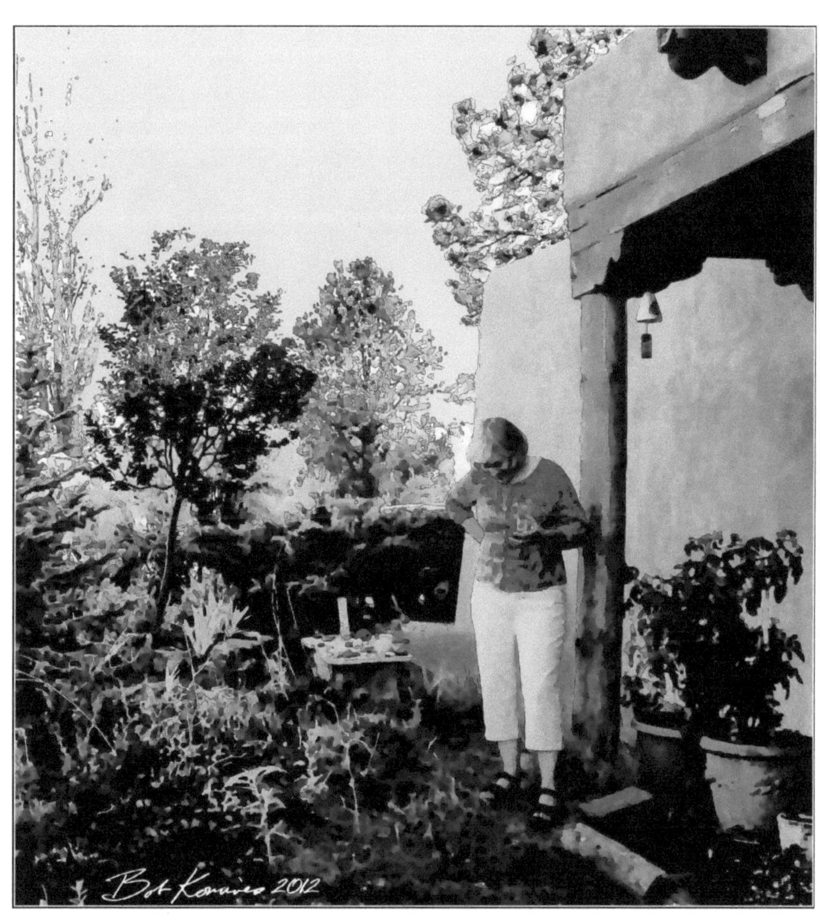

as I feel for a moment long ago,
a moment I scarcely recall
but will never regret.

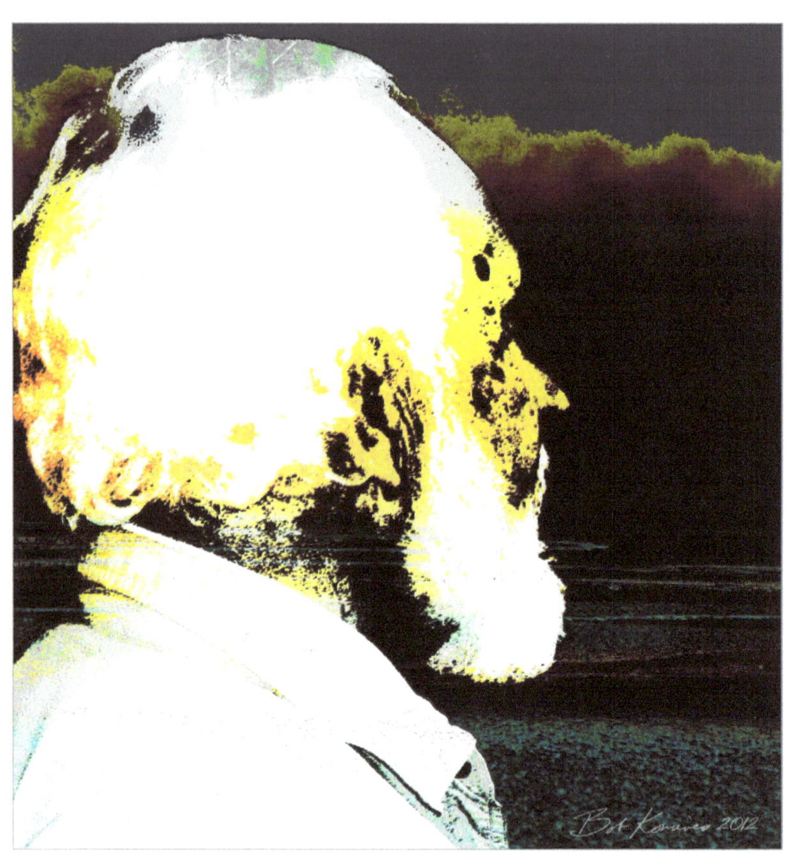

To The Son of Friends

I know what it is to be the younger brother,
though I have never had one older.
I know the peace in mother's arms,
though I am not sure I told her.
I know the rhythm of father's knee
and remember liking warmer milk more than colder.

But, I don't know all the dreams you bring along,
nor all the talents in each finger.
I will be at your side from time to time,
and, if you want, I will linger.

Otherwise,
I leave you on your own
(except for the mother and father you have chosen).
Just permit me a few of a busybody's peeks
and then some of an uncle's devotion.

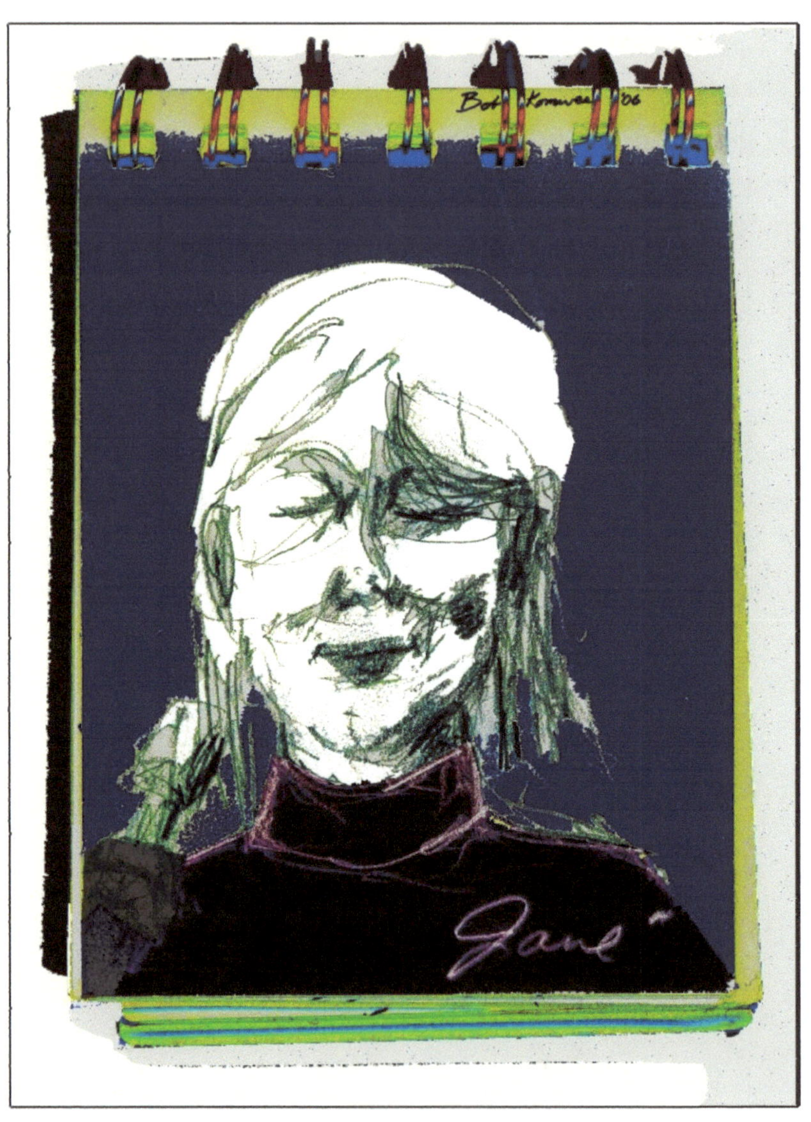
Jane

On the Stairway

"Father,
why am I so much smarter than you? "
(She smiles through my frown.)
"Daughter,
I dropped you on your head one day
while we walked the stairway down."

"*Why do I have much more money than you?* "
(Her eyes give hint of pity.)
"I'm still paying for the violin you forgot
after just three lessons in the city."

"*Will I make the same mistakes as you?* "
(Her jaw seems taut with fear.)
"They'll look quite different from the front
and too much like them from the rear."

"*So, why am I much smarter than you?* "
(Again she smiles and refills my cup.)
"Father dropped me on my head one night
as we walked the stairway up."

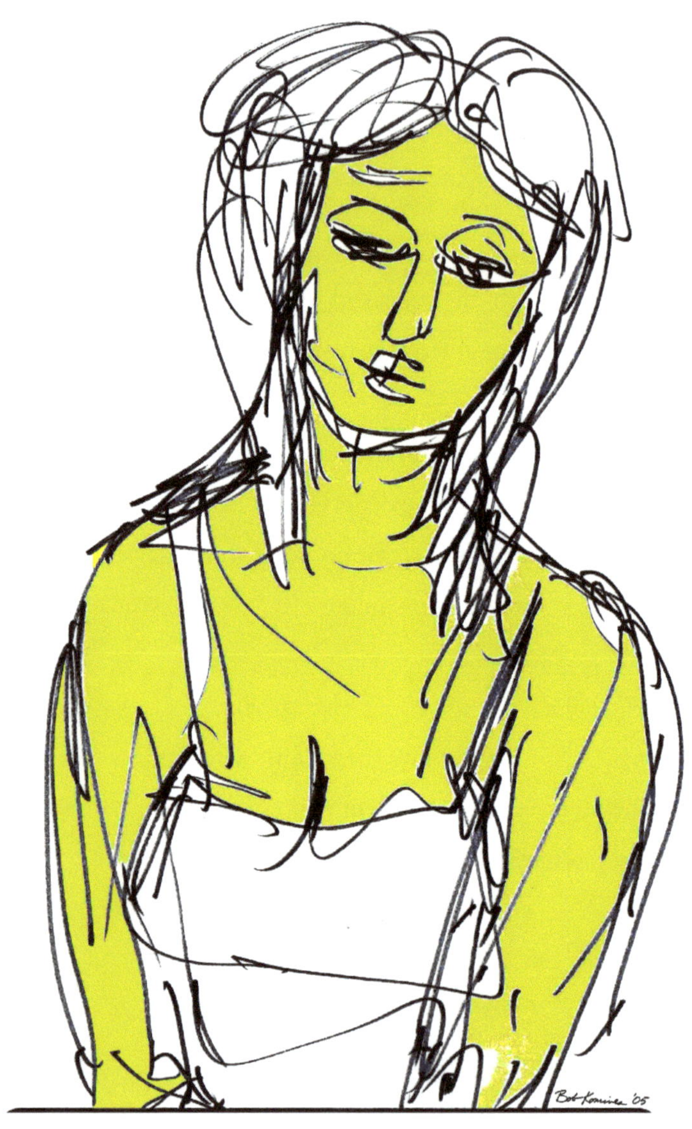

I Must Have Some Secrets

"I must have some secrets," she once told me.
She is still shy—still private.
Good and bad,
she diverts them to a calm lake
somewhere inside.
I say, "Tell me, that's what words are for."
And, at her best,
she may drip out a drop.
She says, "Hug me, I need something more."
And, breast to breast,
I now feel in a flow
that
for
great
volume
force
and
silence
the noise of leaky words
can neither channel nor claim to store.

Hope Cemetery

Do a double-take.
Read this sign again: "HOPE Cemetery"
—clear, bold, and large.

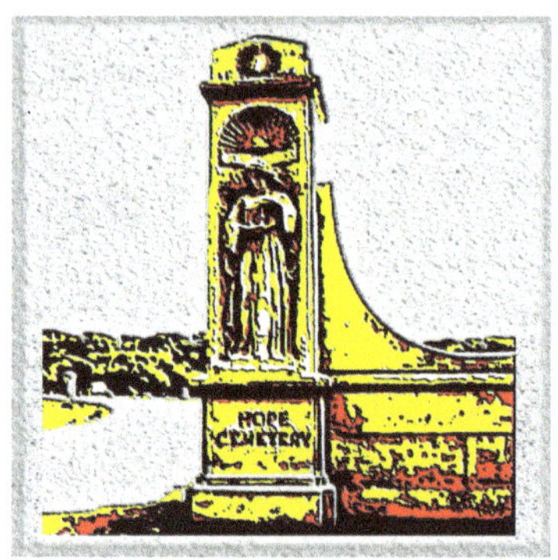

Is it not true?
With death, unanswered questions become answered questions.
What remains for hope's good work?

In life, hope has much to do.
I can live with hope to lose weight,
    but pallbearers will know: I did or I did not.

You and I might hope to get rich.
Will we?—a boring, unanswered question.
Did we? —More interesting, perhaps,

but simply,"no" or "yes."
If alive and already rich, we hope to stay that way.
Yet, beneath a tombstone,
        such hope likely turns to smile or frown.

As to afterlife
(no matter our belief and hope) we can agree
        nobody looks around heaven and says,
        "I hope I get to be here."
In quandary I asked clear-thinking friends for help.
One suggested I misread the sign,
but I have faith in the quality of my double-take.

"Perhaps the message in the name is for us—not them,"
said others.
“As we pass by we remember those who have passed away,
but we should also remember to treasure each day,
appreciate our ancestors, our heritage, the continuity of life.”
I like these thoughts but have difficulty calling them hope.

“It is obvious”,
said another,
“the graveyard is for jerks, scoundrels, miscreants.
Our hope is that they will stay dead.”
I try to be open to this view, but —as city planner—

I think of how such intentional land use would destroy tourism and real estate value.

I warm more to a suggestion that resident graveyard hope need not be profound.
Mundane items that haunt us while alive may persist into our grave. For example:

"I hope I remembered to turn off the gas on the stove."
That thought may well hit coffin-nail on the head.

But yet another suggestion allows me to puzzle no more:

In HOPE Cemetery, hopes do co-mingle.
Both the living and the dead hope
to be remembered well,
to be remembered clearly—
remembered
by those who once explored and opened paths
that remain open before us,
and remembered
by those who will advance or retreat
on paths we leave behind us.

Come To Visit When You Can

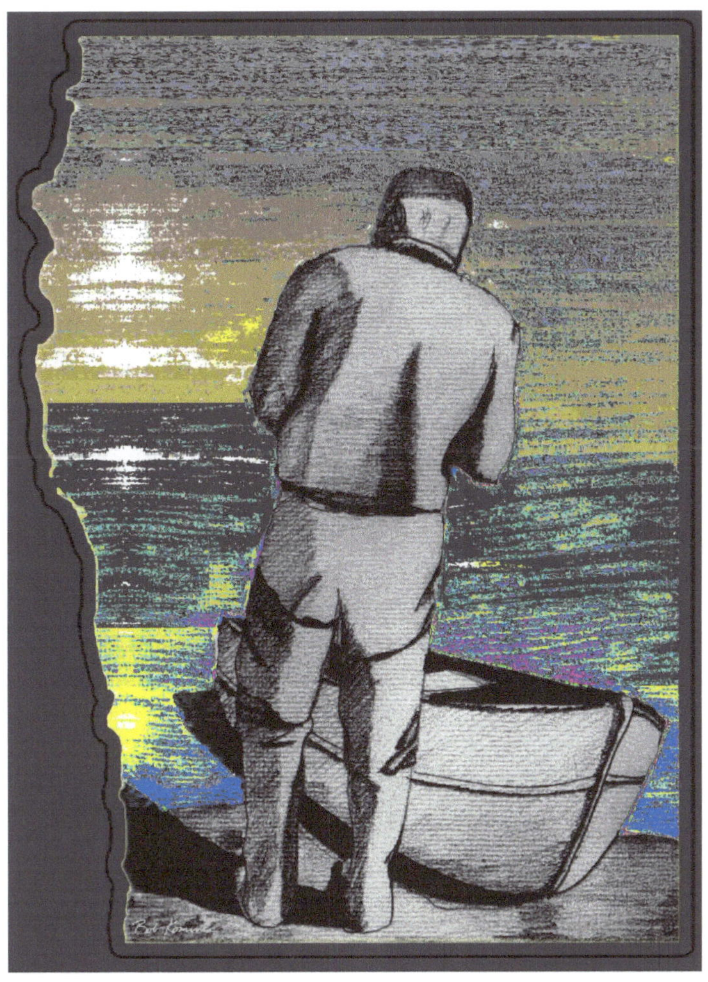

They called me 'PAYT-air' when I was born in Joliet,
"Peter" when I started school in Saint Paul.
Call me Pete.

I have come to rest.
Rest assured I will brag about you.

I was a big kid—
a good student after I learned English.
I had a memory like a trap.
I was a tough kid.
I took nothing from nobody—
not even from my teachers
if I thought they were unfair.
I did not try to treat you all the same.
I did try to treat you fairly.
I was an honest kid.
They could trust me to a penny.
We had about sixteen dollars
when we got married.
Leona raised you kids.
She was a wonderful mother.
I thought I would die first.

Thank you for coming here,
my family,
my friends,
their friends.

Death,

wakes,

funerals,

cemeteries,

they were important in my life.

I was a loyal kid.

I tended flowers
on the graves of brother and sisters.

I earned money taking care of other graves.

Decoration Day was important to me
until they said
we could no longer tend the graves.

I guess this is my heritage.

I hear that a relative,

who does not know how she is related,

tends beautifully

my grandmother's grave in Hungary.

Thank you for coming today,
my family,
my friends,
their friends.

I bragged about each of you

to the others

at one time

and another.

In case you didn't hear it from me,

now is the time to tell each other.

Today, I want you to say

when you shake hands:

"Pete bragged about you."

"Pete bragged about you."

I was strong as a bull.

I was a railway carman,

a center,

a linebacker.

Man, I was lucky!

I never thought life would go so well.

I had a good life.

I built boxcars.

I fixed them,

inspected them.

I liked my job.

I was never afraid to get dirty.
(But, I still clean up pretty good.)

I knew my job.

Nobody knew it better.

I could have been a foreman,
but I didn't want to drag my family
from town to town,
up and down
the Northern Pacific Railway.
I started at the Como Shops.
I was fifteen.
I passed for eighteen.
I was a big kid,
a strong kid.
Thcy wantcd me
to go to Del La Salle high school
to play football.
It would cost four tokens
on the streetcar each day.
I asked my dad.
He said I should get a job.

I never turned down a chance to earn a nickel.
The Depression,
it was tough for everyone.
I helped build Monkey Island
at Como Zoo on the W.P.A.

I don't like social workers.

She wouldn't give me money

to buy a white shirt

so I could tend bar.

She gave me money for coal.

I bought the shirt.

Leona and I collected our coal
along the railroad tracks.

The Swede fired the other bartender.

He gave me a raise for the extra money
he found in the till when I worked.

I underbid a man and a mule
to dig a house foundation by hand.

I didn't know much,

but I was never afraid to ask advice—
from the Irishman,
the Swede,
the Jew

the Polack.

The Kraut taught me to read a newspaper.
(If you want to know, I'll tell you.)

Each of you taught me something.

I passed it on.

You asked my advice.

I gave it—much more than you wanted.

But, take it or leave it.

I don't want to tell you how to live your life.

I had a good life.

I was lucky.

I made some good decisions.

(No stockbroker ever tried twice
to give me advice I hadn't asked for.)

We moved to the lake.

Man, Leona was happy.

I was a tough man to live with.

I made mistakes.

I expected to die first.

After forty years together

she gave me a big hug and said,
"Pete, I guess I want to live with you."

I suppose that says something.

I got my high-school equivalency
at age sixty.

I liked my work,

but I retired early.

Everything just fell into place.

Those were good years.

Except the lake kept rising.

With a wheelbarrow we moved
truckloads of fill.

We were both strong.

I was strong.

I loved my flowers.

I loved my vegetables.

I can tell you how
to get a long harvest from your broccoli.

There is a right way to do most things.

If it's worth doing

it's worth doing right!

I always said, "I'm as good as the best
and better than the rest,"

but I never said I was perfect.

I made mistakes.

I told you so.

So, don't do as I did;
do as I said.

We sent you kids to Catholic school,

but it was you kids who got Leona and me

to go to church every Sunday.

I hope I thanked you for that.

I had no problem making up my own mind
as to what is right
and what is wrong.
I hope you can thank me for that.

I was a tough old man,
but I often said, thank you.
Remember that.
You never did get me to stop swearing,
or to change my grammar.
You can't take off all the rough edges.

I led a rough life when I was a young man.
I hung around with some bad characters.
Sitting on a boxcar,
I told the Polack I was tired of it.
I wanted to settle down.
I met Leona.
She was ready too.
I thought I would die first.

We had a good life,
but my last seven years were tough.

The last three years have been tough—
tough on me,
tough on you.
I had had a memory like a trap.
I was a strong man.
I vacuumed the floor,
made breakfast and lunch
while Leona fished.
I read my newspapers,
my magazines.
I liked to study before I made a decision.
It worked for us.
We paid our way—
even today.

I never wanted to be dependent.
But, you could depend on me,
and I could depend on you.
That's what family and friends are for.

I bragged to each of you about the other.
Remember me and tell each other.
Plant a flower in my name.
Come to visit when you can.

Call me Pete.

I have come to rest.

Rest assured I will brag about you.

was a great one

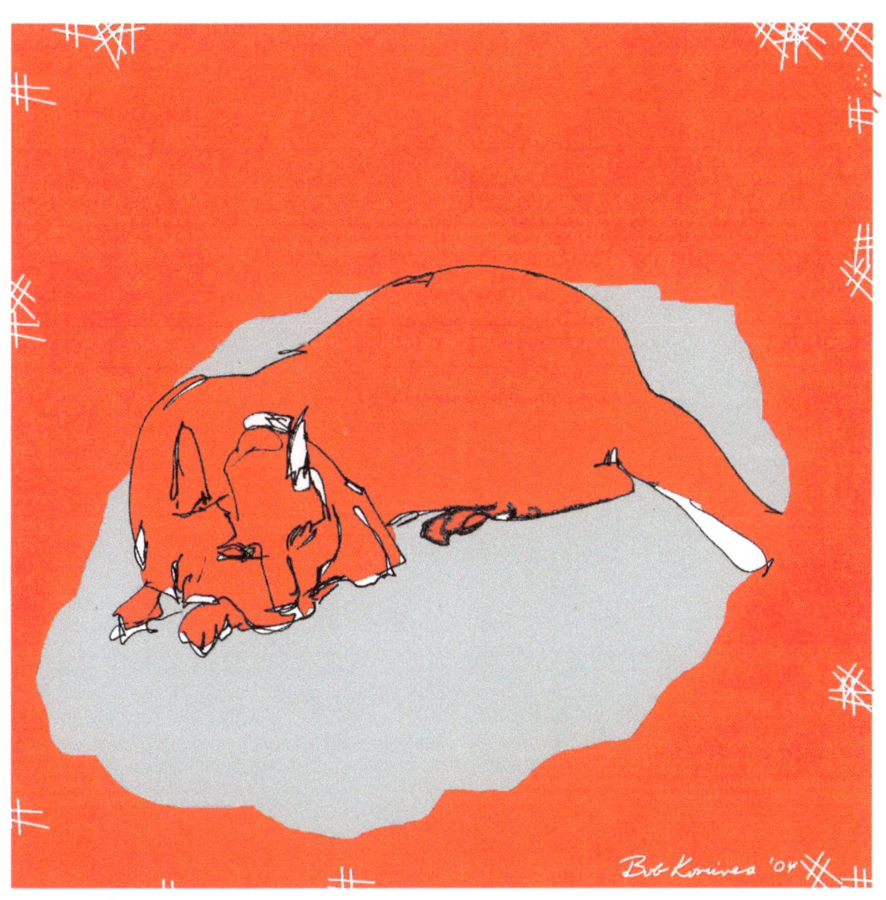

If I Were a Perfect Cat

If I were a perfect cat,
    good as good can be,
would I breed and feed a neighborhood of kittens
    and teach them to love and worship me?
Perhaps I would,
    but I would be selfish—
    I would not be as good as a good cat can be.

What is lovable about my master?
    I call him Mister Supreme.
Yes, he took me in;
he fed and sheltered me—
    but that is easy enough for the all-powerful.
Indeed, he is good to me—
    but that he should be.
He has that obligation.
It is he who chose to bring me in,
and he who expects me to be the perfect cat.

You Think Galileo Was a Great One

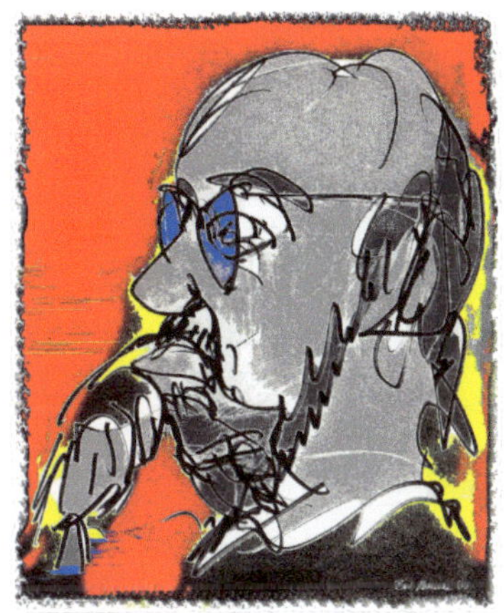

You think Galileo was a great one.
but he wrote heresy in 1632.
He wrote, " Copernicus is right,
our earth circles the sun,
not the other way around. "
You think Galileo was a great one,
but in 1633 he did recant
so he would not burn.

Now you too believe
that to the sun belong the planets,
that we live on one example of them,
our sun-centered revolution,

a scientific revelation,
from a genius then among them,
a religious revolution,
insult to god above them.

One way or another,
believers go early, but truth stays late.

Yes, die for your country
to get a plaque.
Yes, die for your religion
to get guaranteed heaven.
But why die for your science
to get guaranteed hell?
Why should you burn for your solar system?
Is the martyr more hero than the genius?
We well know how to make you a martyr,
but we lack the weapon to make you a genius.

How can you resist?
How can you insist:
that Earth is a sphere,
if it is healthier to talk "flat"?
that we came from evolution,

if the inquisition favors special creation?
that all peoples are equal,
if we preach one-ethnic perfection?

Recant today so you will not burn.
Choose humbly to not believe what you believe.
Humility is a sign of greatness.
For everybody knows
and the Bible humbly shows
our Earth to be center to the universe.

You think Galileo was a great one
for finding the motion of the pendulum,
the equal rates of falling objects,
and, of course, our telescope.
But then he wrote that Copernicus is right.
You think Galileo was a great one
—but then he did recant
—but then he did not burn.

Little by Slowly

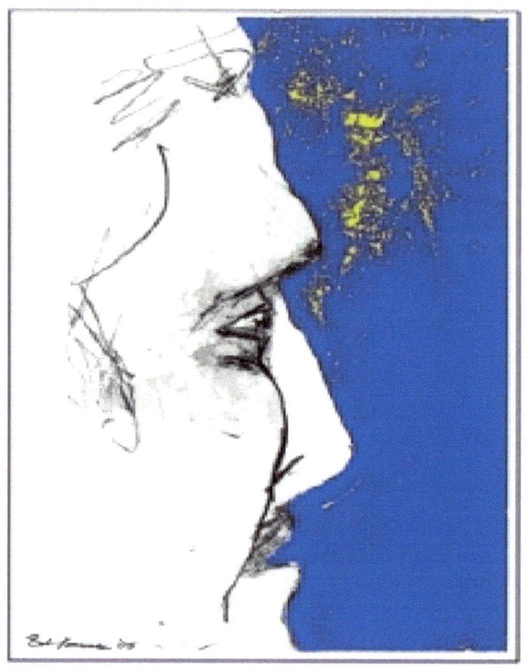

I inch upward
little by slowly
from this ledge
near bottom
in this abyss
where earth gave way beneath me—
dropping further than I thought my land could drop.

I look up,
see a climb that will outlive me,
take notice in the dim
of varied walls and sides surrounding:
good sides,
bad sides,
sides with sheared and slippery walls,
sides where I could sculpt and garden,
sides where (little by slowly)
others climb.
They rise from below me.
They lead the way—way above me.
They pause alone to sculpt and garden.
Little by slowly
I shall climb to those nearby:
to those who will outlive abyss,
to those who will pull and push my old bones,
to those who need my stubbornness,
and to those who will feast from my memory
of what was earth above
before collapse.

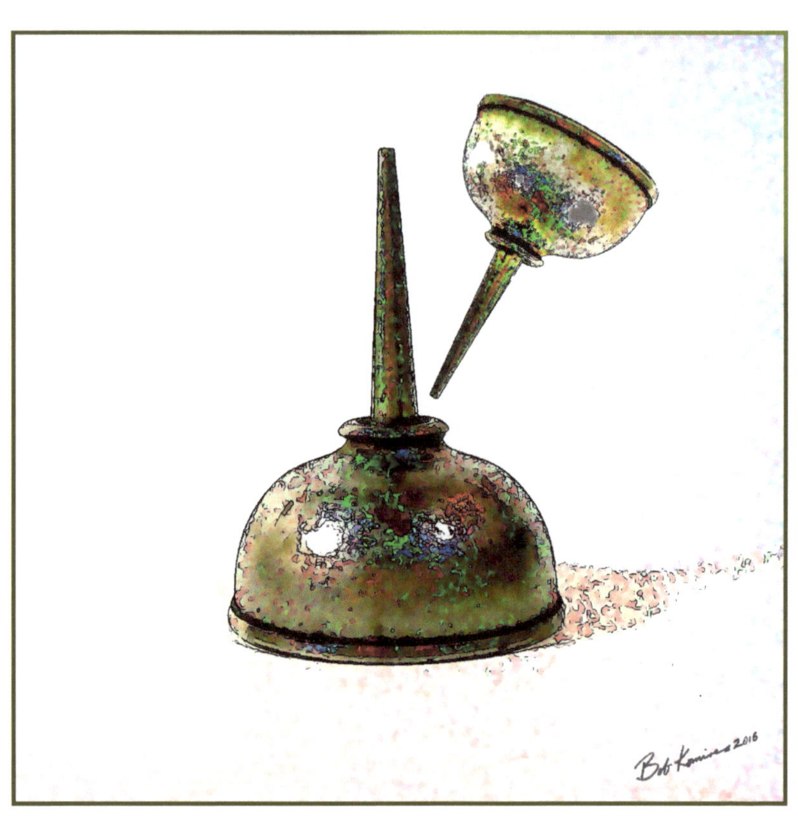

Beauty's laws

Beauty's laws we partially know
by their refusal to obey our own
unwilling to be always sensible
nor nonsensical
humble
nor august
Each is silent, yet articulate
simultaneous, but free of babble
timeless and immediate

Ode to Bollard

Oh, Bollards; Oh, Bollards.
Pillars of my community.
Through old-town alley and downtown street,
past art and fun,
in winter cold and summer heat,
you guide me,
protect me.
For my comings out and my goings in
you keep me out of harms way.
Yet, do I notice? Do I say?
"Thank you, Bollard,"
or even: "Bollard, good day!"
No, Bollard; No, Bollards.
At least, not until today
when you helped me walk
to museum (that has genius on display),
to old town's square,
then by that place of children at play.
You kept me from
traffic's hazards,

ugly's dumpsters,
then guided me on to hardware store
for errand of the day.

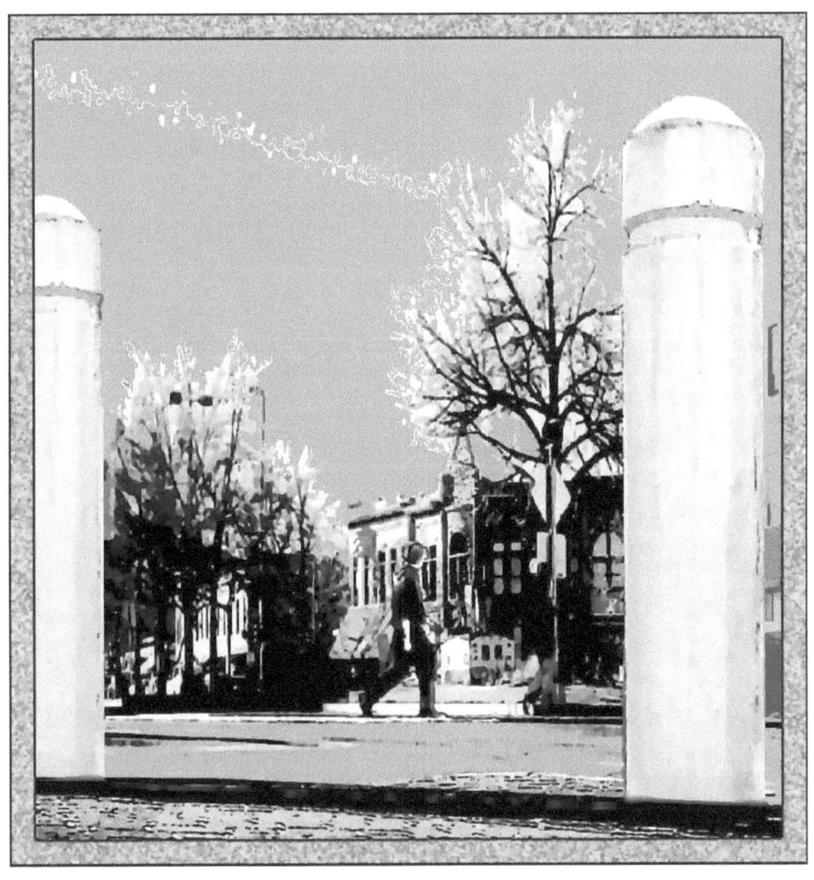

Oh, Bollard; Oh, Bollards.
Where buildings loom tall and cubical,
(where straight streets abound)

you too stand straight, but

short,

humble,

round.

Oh, Bollards; Oh Bollards.

While you are too noticed and familiar to

Canis

lupus

familiaris

you are visibly invisible,

unfamiliar

ignored,

alien to

Homo

sapiens

sapiens.

Oh, Bollards; My Bollards.

Pillars of my protection.

Please take notice of my notice;

please accept my affection.

Out My Backdoor

You'll hear me say

it takes three days

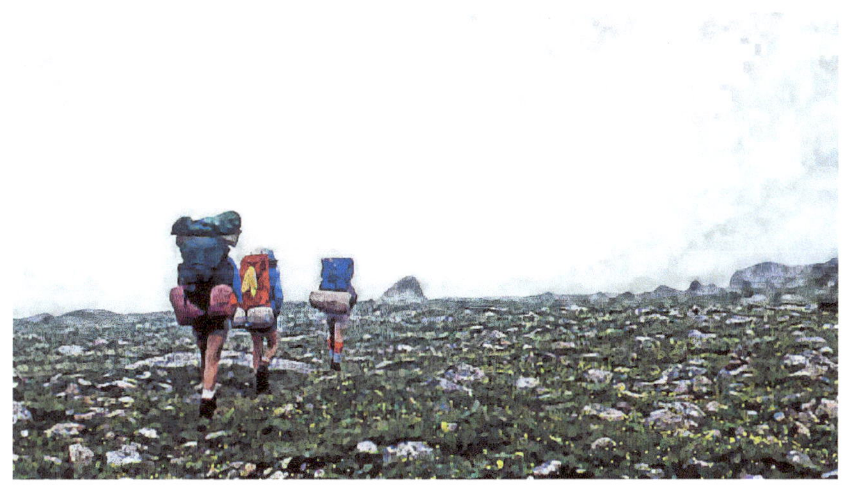

out my back door

to the middle of the wild,

And so I did,

as he cleared my way to his grinding wheel.

You'll find that among your new neighbors

we borrow and lend in a neighborly way.

No payment offered and none accepted,

yet, you might say,

one is always expected.

The price to borrow one thing
is to remember to ask for two.
We lend a tool freely
where we can send along our wisdom.
Your question may be short or long,
as fits the subject,
but the answer should never be so short
as to end before you turn to leave.
Thus, our advice will often run full limit—
just twice what the fetching
        and lending need take.

After my first winter, and half a summer,
this custom had already served me well.
Being the youngest and the newest,
I lacked tools
        and had need for everyday advice.
A few houses over,
the pruning saw hung near his head
as I walked through the workshop door.
"How long does it take
  to get into the back country from here?"
He said nothing

until he had lowered the saw
        and put it into my hand.
Well, if you want to hear how I figure it,
(I paused near the door to listen.)
it takes me no more than an hour and a half;
only the canyon sits in my way.

Across the alley,
she walked with me to her shed
to fetch the garden fork.
"How long does it take
  to get into the back country from here?"
She may have wished
        I had asked about her tomatoes.
We inspected them going and halfway back.
'depends on how you see it.
But I suppose I'd say, it takes me three hours
out my back door and into the wilderness—
to close the door,
drive up the canyon,
put on my pack,
and trek a few miles up the trail.
She reconfirmed as I latched the gate.

Yes, I guess it's three hours
that join this place,
my chosen life,
with my mountain escape of choice.

I needed only to go next door
to sharpen my mower blade.
"How long does it take
  to get into the back country from here?"
He had just begun to change the spark plugs
in his pickup on the far side of the garage.
You'll hear me say
it takes three days
out my back door
to the middle of the wild,
And so I did,
as he cleared my way to his grinding wheel.
With several minutes of grinding ahead of me
he could afford to confuse me in the beginning.

Of course, I hinted that among his neighbors
an hour and a half, or perhaps three hours,
were thought to be enough.

Those are honest folks,
but, you might say,
I speak in the sense of senses.
Now, my sense of smell
and my sense of taste,
they could agree
with those lower estimates.
One breath of mountain air
inhaled deeply through my nose
places me right back in the wilderness.
There, any food, lightly carried,
tastes as good as I care to expect.
But, ear, eye, and touch
do not fit in so quickly.
I hear beauty;
I see it; I touch it—
even before I exhale
that first mountain breath.
Yet those senses flit about,
not always knowing new from old,
nor together from apart.
They keep referring back here
to this life—

enjoying so much the difference

that you might say,

they miss out

on much of the difference.

Then, some moment

(expected but briefly unexpected)

around a trail bend

on my third day out,

I make it all the way back

to the middle of the wild—

all of me,

five senses,

together in one place.

While he got lost in thought

I finished up my grinding

and put the clutter back where it had lain.

Then I sent back a nod of understanding

as I took away his final words.

Now, before you reject my estimate,

let me tell you, it is not all bad.

On that last day,

I put on my pack

and walk down

out of the back country,

leaving that back door wide open.

Then I drive on down the canyon

knowing that

for at least three more days

parts of me will stay up there

in the middle of the wild.

So, welcome to our neighborhood.
That yard sure has needed care.
Ah, there's that damned long-handled spade!
I'm sorry for the delay.
'haven't used it since last fall.
You can see it is still quite sharp.
It will always be here when you need it.

And, before you leave,
since you asked my advice,
I'd say you should take that hoe of yours next door.
It could use a little sharpening
to tame those weeds in the alley.

I see him there in his garage
    tuning up his van.
He came back down just yesterday.
Go on over,
but take care in what you ask.
He may still lack a few of his senses.

Untitled, 4-Lines

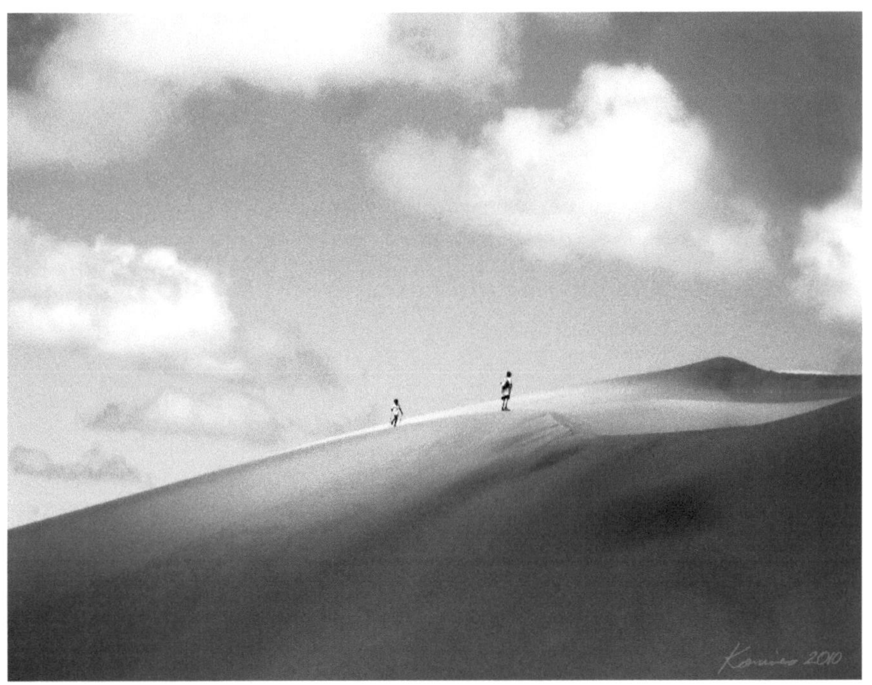

When morning is singular
amid beauties too numerous
let me be humble
let me be proud.

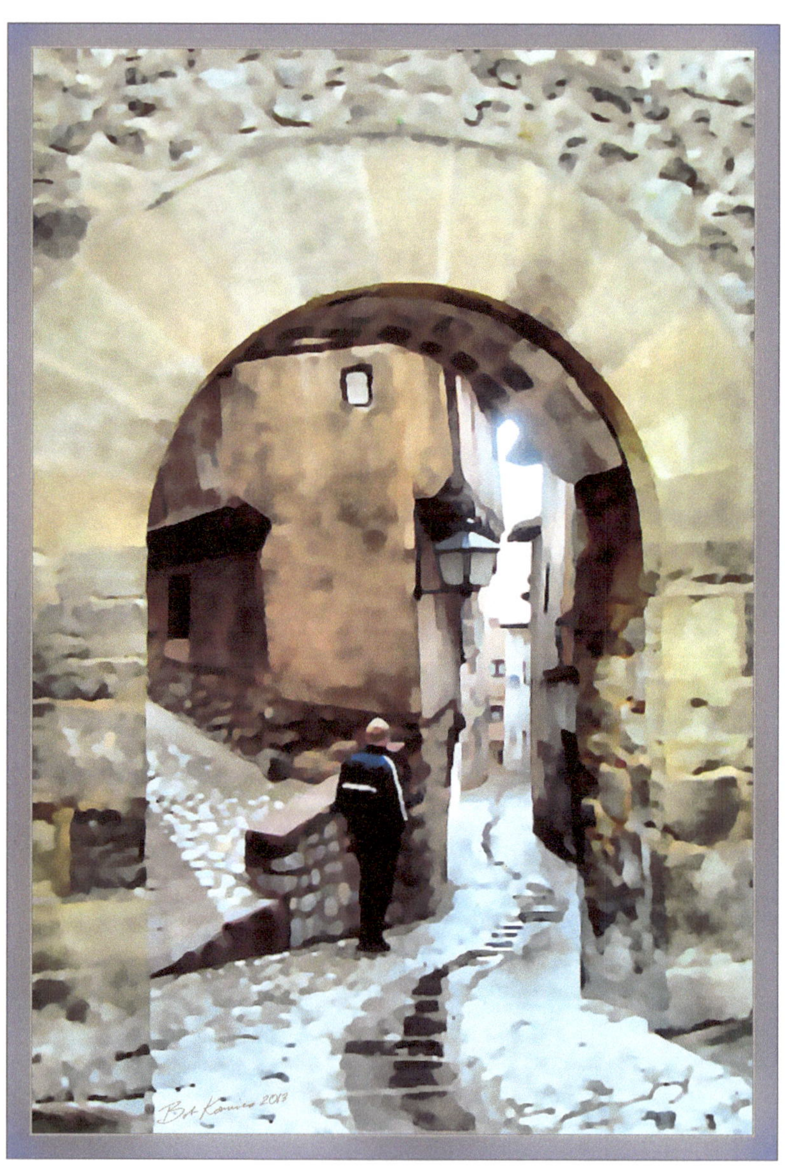

Special Places

Special places
are where I always go
for my peace,
for my excitement.
They are places
I have yet to be
that yet wait to grab me,
and places to which I cannot return
—except in thought.
Most sit fixed;
some float free;
home need only be my family.
Special places
are sometimes spaces,
some places time,
sometimes wine,
someplace lonely in this mind of mine,
sometimes everyday,
sometimes new,
sometimes little,
sometimes much,
sometimes solely in the touch of you.

anklets & friends

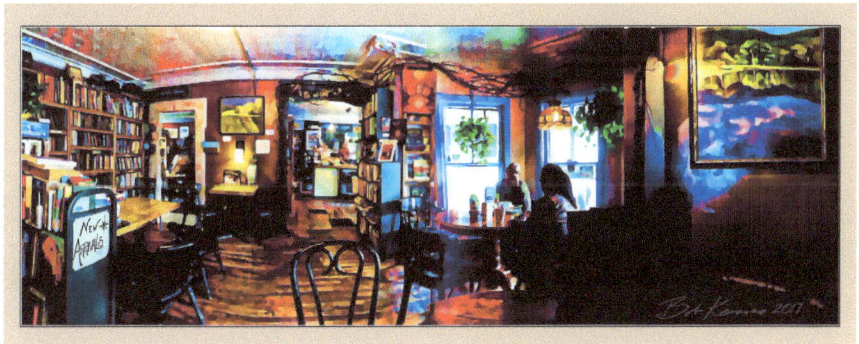

Collaboration with Art-full Friends

Let us imagine art-full bookmark
to send and ascend
from art-full friend to friend.
Let it deepen our depths
as we
converse
convert
converge
then pause together
at art-full end
to emerge
each alone
more art-full friend.

Benches of Herceghút

Yes, these are pretty flowers.
Does not every village have such flowers?
We have two hundred simple houses,
two hundred root cellars,
three hundred wine cellars,
and two simple churches;
but no castle,
no museum.
Everyone will wonder why you wandered by.

.

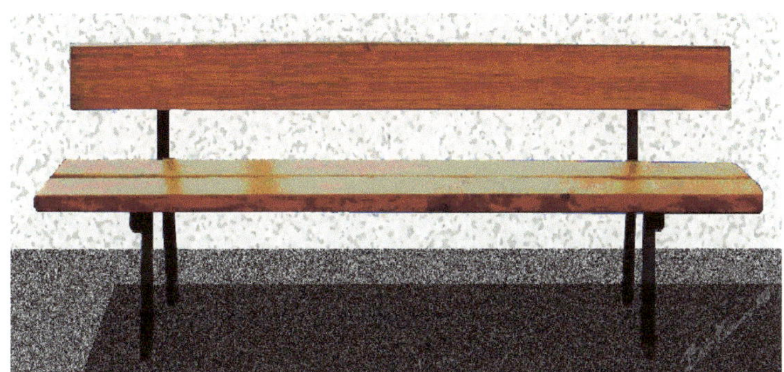

Yes, this is my bench.
Does not every village have such benches?

We sit in front of our houses,
in front of our fences,
facing out,
along the walk,
looking over our flowers to the street,
looking after each other,
watching for you.
Can there be village without benches?
Why have flowers but no bench to sit on?
Why have neighbors but no benches
for them to wander by?

Yes, I sit here when my work is done.
Should not everyone have such a bench?
I sit here to rest,
speak to my neighbors,
enjoy my flowers and today's best story.
I speak here from my wisdom,
from my prejudice.
I sat here with each of my babies
on display for all to see.

I teach each grandchild to sit here,
say hello,
and kiss an elder's hand.
I watch,
and I remember to tell my neighbors who has
come by while they were hard at work.
I return your smile,
answer your greeting,
and wonder why you would have no bench
yet have interest in mine.
Here, fifty neighbors pass on bicycle and foot
while the others stand hard by their work
or sit upon benches to look.
They will wonder.
They will wonder until I tell them
why you wandered by.

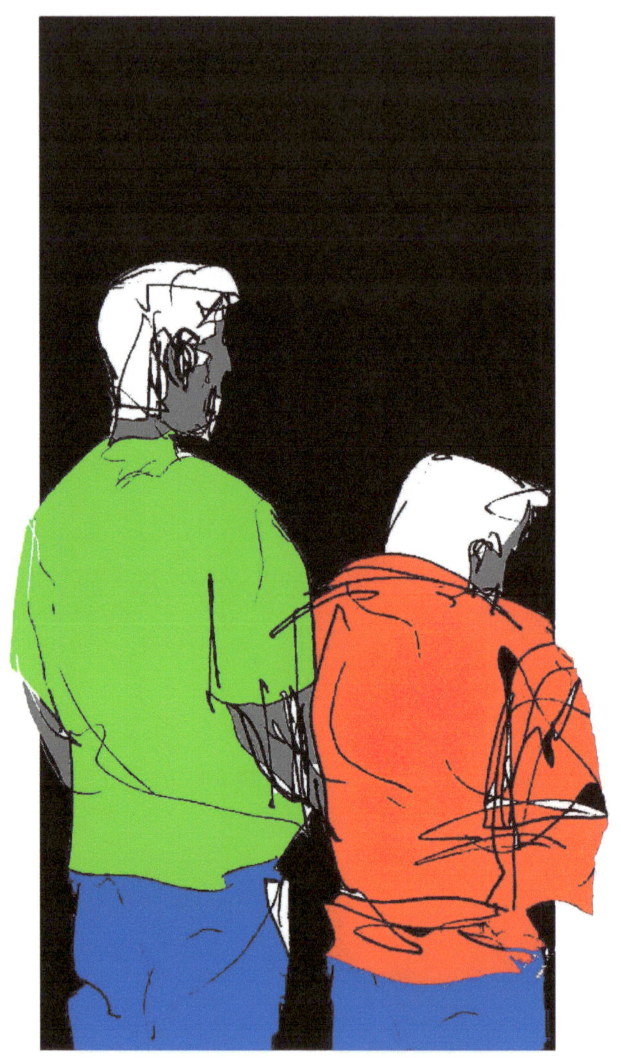

A Wish

That
for three hundred days
I notice I am alive.
This is much of my wish for a perfect year.

Then,
for five robust thanksgivings
and five dozen days
to pause
as I celebrate that a friend was born.

Thanksgiving Week

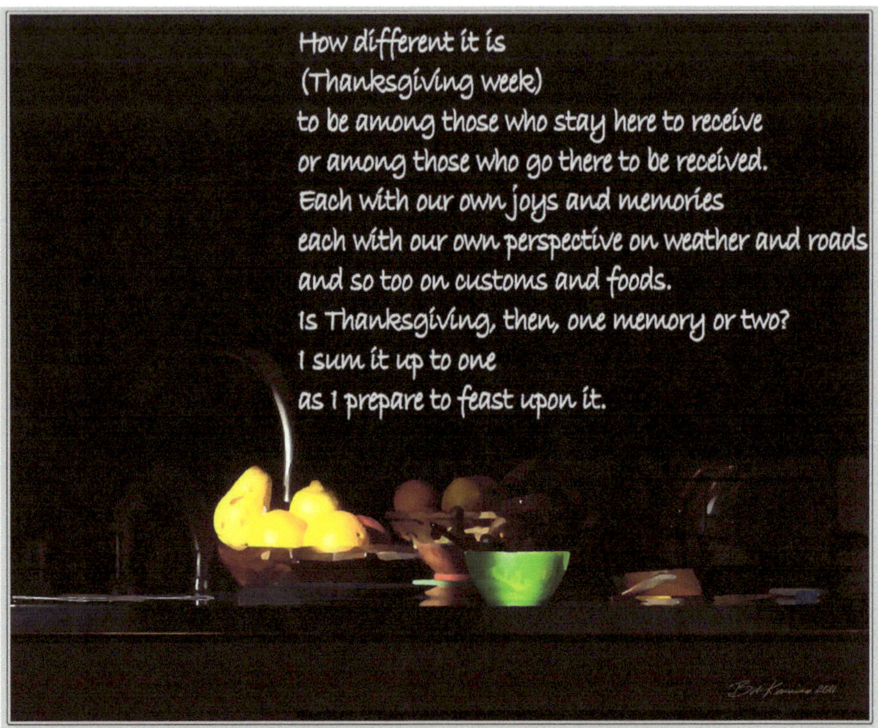

Is This Table Free?

“Is this seat free?”

“Szabad?”

“¿Está Libre?

“Is this table free?”

I ponder
the friendships;
marriages, affairs, businesses, partnerships;
transfers of tickets, newspapers, books, magazines
that begin with such question.

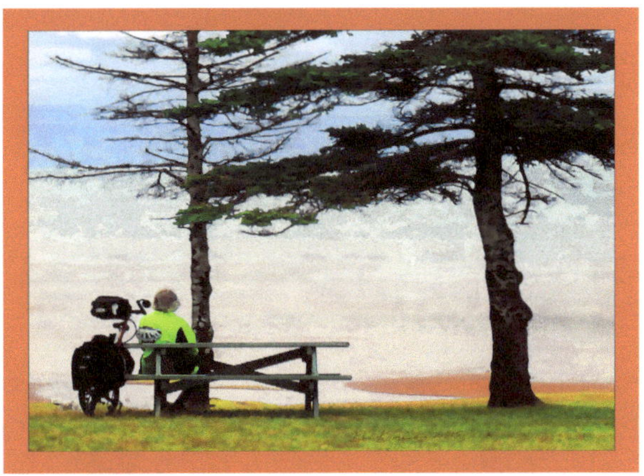

In my life?
Perhaps none, exactly,
but, some important ones
to be inexact.

My path into marriage begins
where an angry girl says:
"I want you to get your drunken friend off my seat!"
That was on one of the last 20th-Century-Limiteds
racing west beneath Lake Erie.

My discovery of relatives in Fertoszentmiklós
begins when I enter a 2-table coffee house
and say (unconsciously, but aloud):
  "Nincs szabad asztal."
  "There is no free table."

I begin a friendship
when I find there to be no room (to stand nor sit)
to hear a panel discussion.
  "No room?", ask I
from within a crowd of the disappointed.
And then, ask I:
  "Anyone want to watch basketball instead?"
from the depths of my ambivalence.

“I do!”
responds fellow enthusiast, new friend,
from somewhere behind.

I believe
(given a gift of perfect recall)
(in some room in my brain)
(across a broad tabletop)
I could sort and recover other memories
of when something like
“Is-this-seat-free?”
opens a chapter of my life.

Lacking such gift,
(synaptic tabletops otherwise occupied)
“Nincs szabad asztal.”

Something Difficult Has Taken Your Smile

Something difficult has taken your smile.
I need not know what,
nor need I know how nor when.
Neither must you nor should you force your lips
to pretend that radiance
when you
see me
see you.
Because you cannot see
that my pain equals yours when you try.

Nor should you question my readiness to listen
(to give silent embrace)
there
where you may summon me,
or here
where I will welcome you,
if you wish,
when you wish,
as you wish.

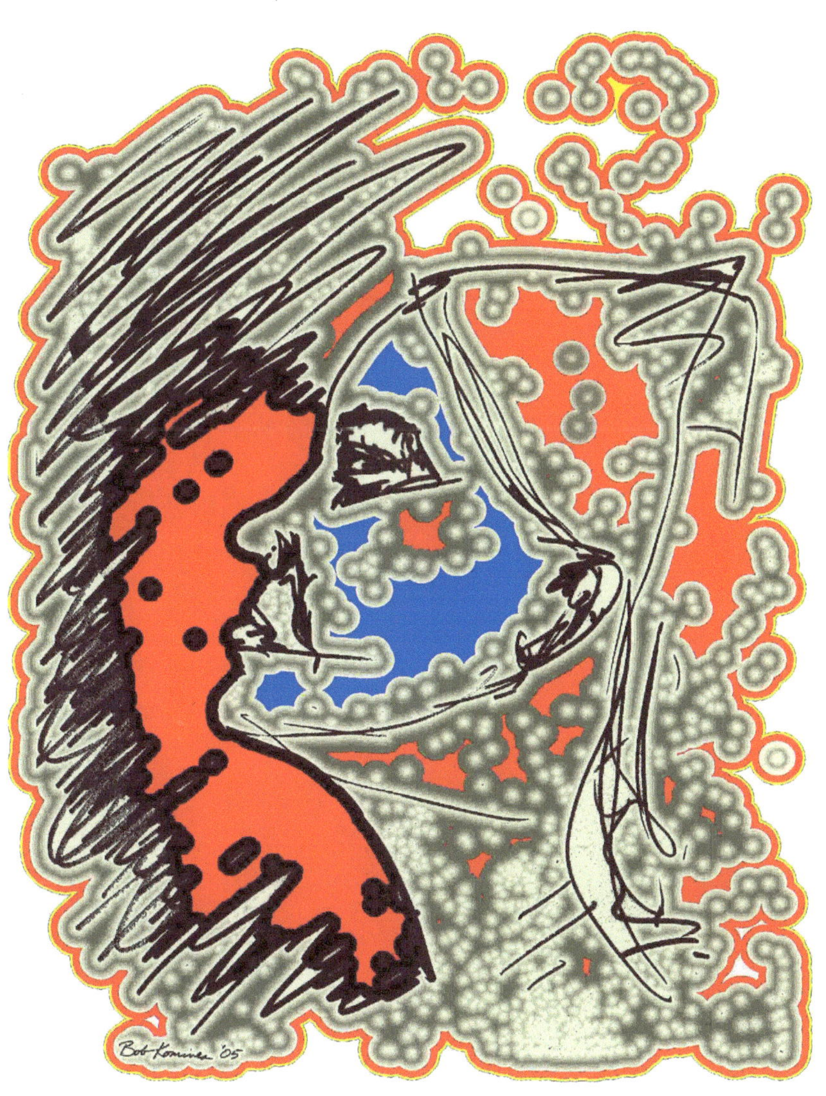

Stools

on
stools
along
bar
sit
drinker
stranger
lover
friend
strung
together
strung
together
together
strung
end
to
end

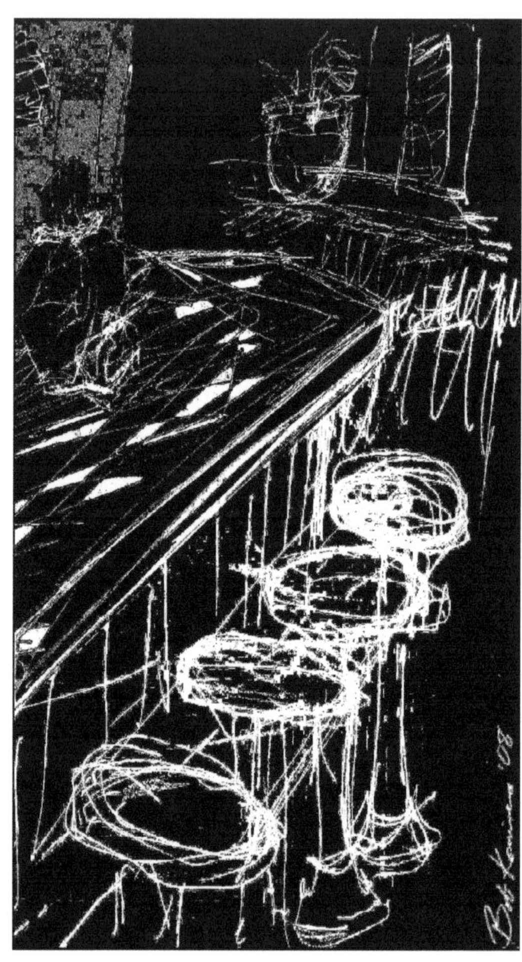

Valerie

I joined you, dear friend, at Valerie's bedside. From
that visit (nine years and nine hundred miles
distant) I returned home to draft lines for a poem
that was to begin:
"How well do I know Valerie?"

I know not why I failed to finish that poem.
Perhaps it is that she recovered so beautifully,
as she had done often before,
and would repeat several times more.
I remember well why I had to begin her poem
with a question.
How can I feel so close to person
with whom I have spent so little time?
How can I feel attached to her children
whom I have hardly met
and might not recognize on the street?
Much is due to you.
Over brief summers and a short year, you became
my great and open friend.

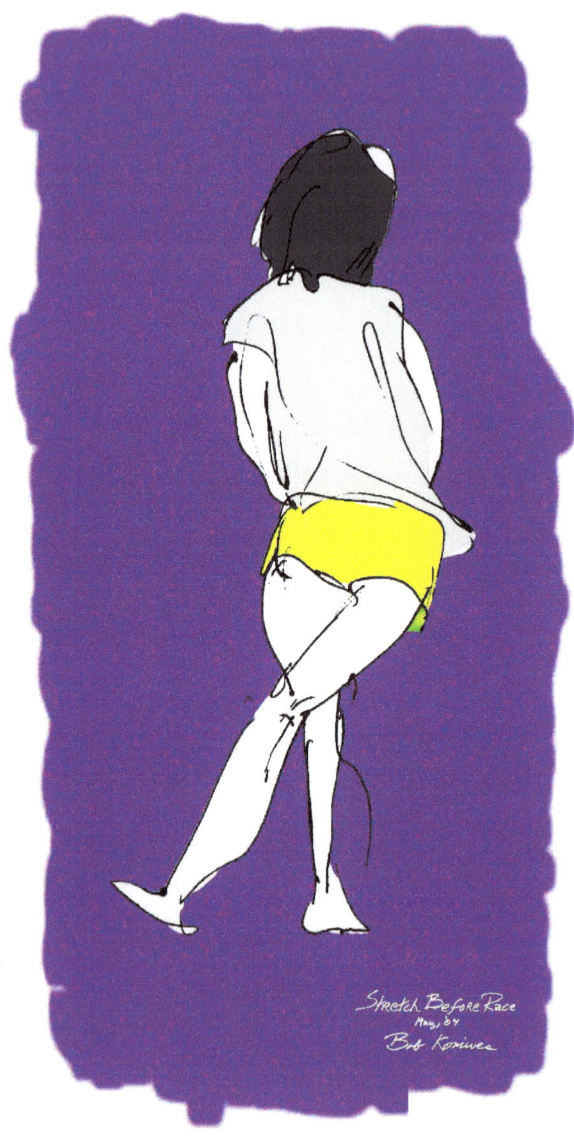
Stretch Before Race
May, '84
Bob Komives

If that were not enough, you married a woman who
embraced me and my family with old-friendship
from the moment we met.

I remember that moment of meeting.
You and I and a few other young men
sat in our car, stopped in traffic,
nearing the football game.
Across the street, two pedestrians passed
headed to the stadium.
Everybody but I recognized the tall, beautiful girl
and paid no attention to her date.
For, ignoring a recent quarrel,
they knew she was your girlfriend.
Valerie looked over,
recognized, and, with coy smile,
excused herself to her date
as she walked to our motionless car.
Never have I seen more adept display of warm and
cool, receptivity and reserve, vulnerability and
strength, friendliness and dignity.
I was charmed.

It was clear to me
    that this lover's quarrel must end
    (or, I suppose, continue lovingly indefinitely)
    for your sake and mine.

Perhaps we can best testify who,
    in the decades since that Saturday,
    saw Valerie so little.
So quickly a long-interrupted conversation would
    return to the important, difficult,
    and humorous aspects of life,
    as if there had been no gap of years.
She walked gently on a plain
    that seemed above the rest of us,
    yet she would elevate us above herself.

How well did I know Valerie?
I feel that a few times I knew her well,
but never, dear friend,
did I know her well enough.

Law of Anklets and Chain

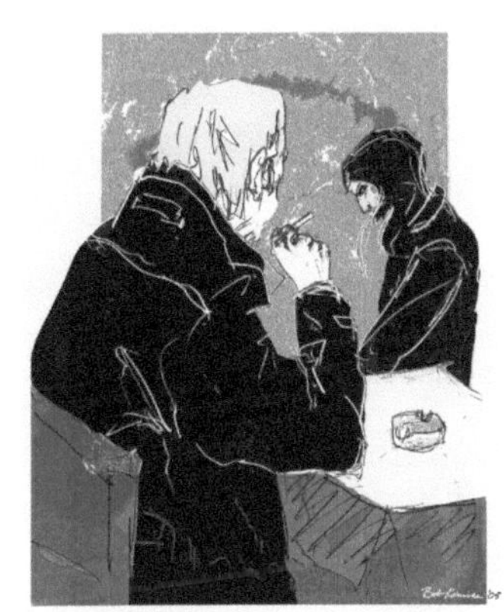

Everywhere on earth
(Wisconsin included)
Government is unsainted.
Unions are unsainted.
Business,
Industry,
Marketplace and Mall,
Friends and Neighbors,
Poets, Pagans, Priests and Preachers,
Farmers, Foresters and Fishers,
Up-staters,
Down-staters,
High-rollers and Good-waiters,
Peter, Paula, Grace and Paul:
They are unsainted.
Yet,
because there are anklets aplenty
and only one chain,
to hell with one
is to hell with us all.

Falls A Road Steeply

Here falls a road steeply from hillside mothers

that borrows its way from down-washing streams.

Here falls a steep cornfield to hillside fathers

that pays out its earth to down-washing streams.

Here falls a rain harshly on hillside children

that charges down slopes

and washes down dreams.

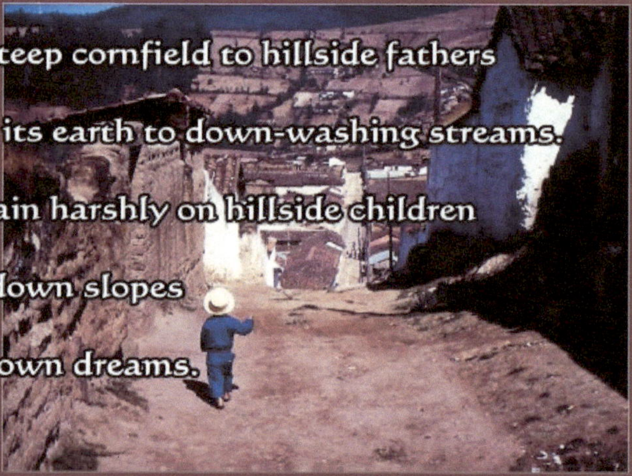

Night's Sound of Rain

Night's sound of rain
    on roof and skylight
calls back rhythm
    on tin-tile-thatch,
    on canvas-nylon-wood
    on twigs and leaves—
        old and new.

Night's sound of rain
calls upon concern
    for those who want tomorrow dry,
brings celebration
    with those who crave it moist,
brings new and repeat anticipations.

Night's sound of rain anticipates
    morning's first step outside,
    impossible to remember smells
        of vitality and growth,

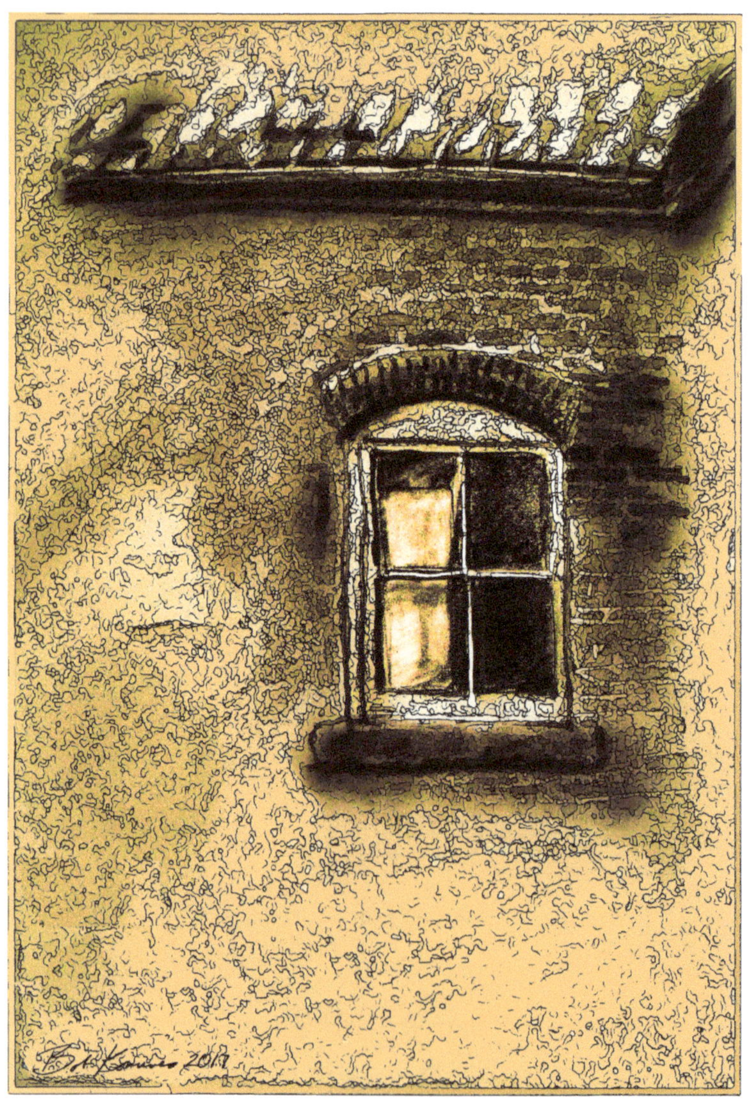

of burstings and birth,
of aging, disrepair, and putrefaction,
of renewal,
and of perfumes that beauty hides when dry.

Come.
Come.
The hour has come.

Rise up to it!

Why I Speak

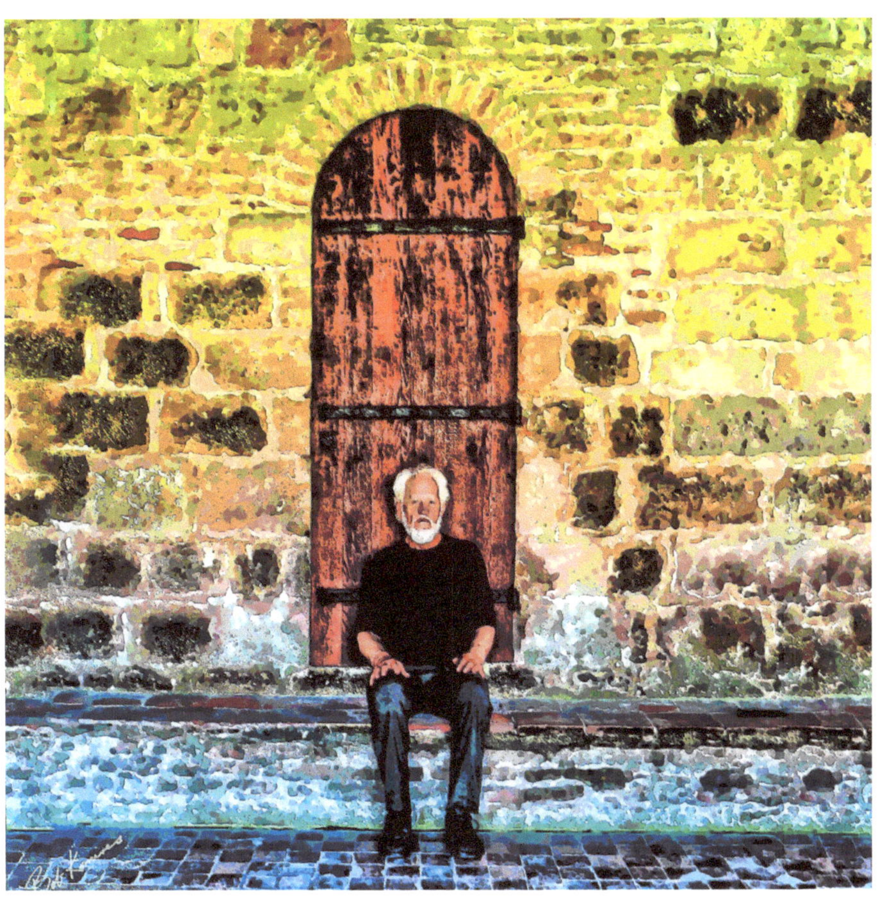

Before

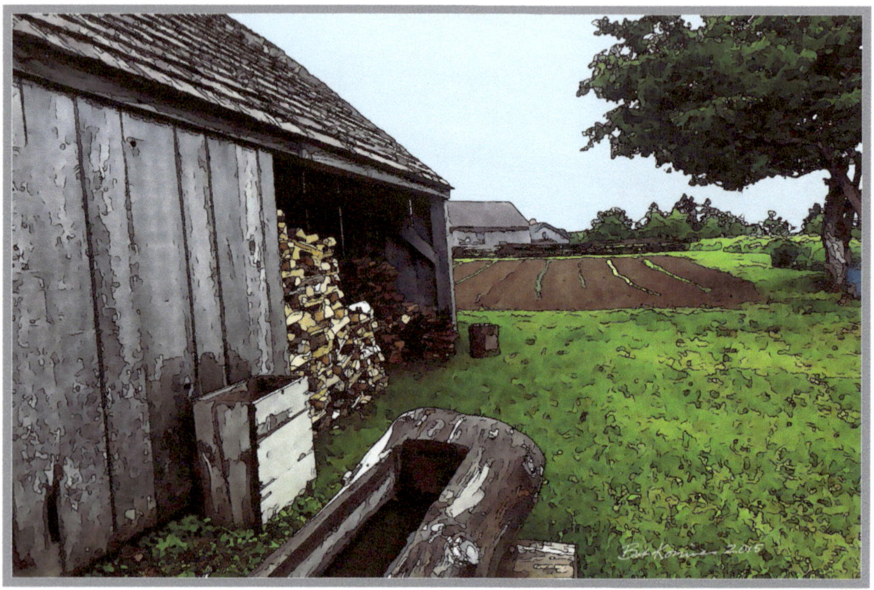

Before his invention,
before her inspiration,
before they saved humankind,
rescued our fauna and flora,
freed our spirit and body from misery,
before this glorious history,
before all this
came their floundering,

their flailing,
their drifting from dreams dreamt
to dreams lost,
from past failure to again failing.
Before fame,
before success,
lonely toil,
dogged quest.

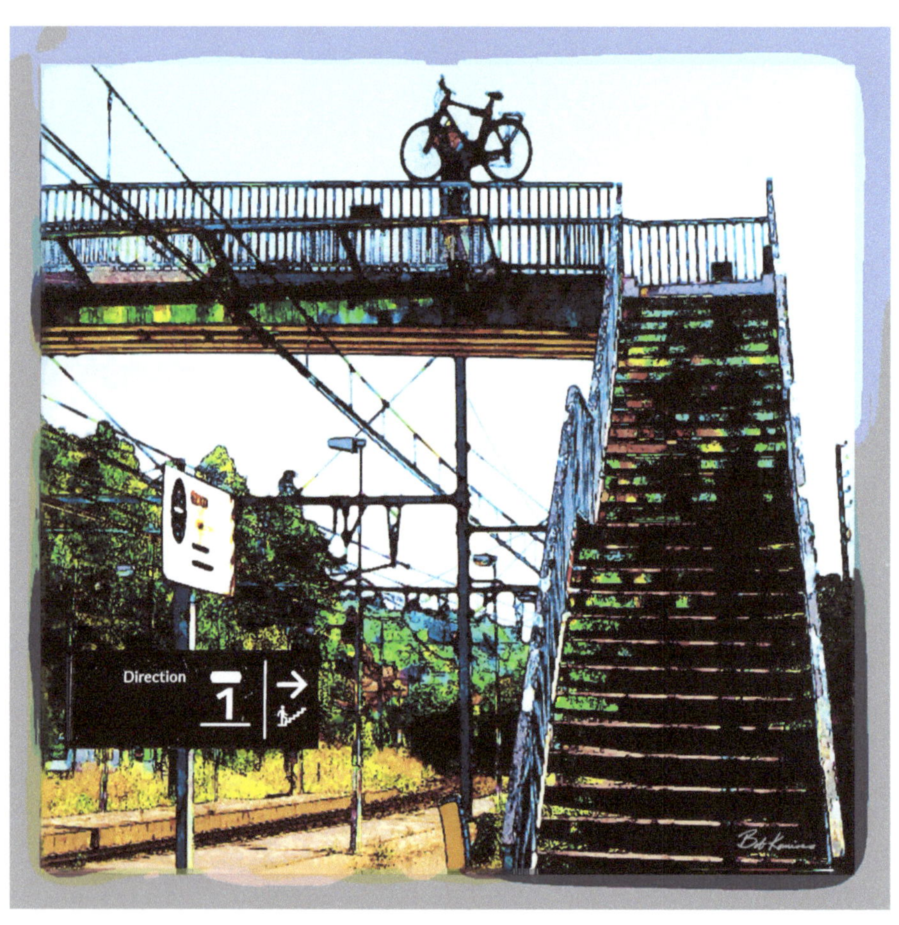
Direction
1

You Say You Want To Simplify

Draft 1

You say you want to simplify;
life is too hectic,
pressured,
insane.
You yearn for less,
so you detest the new, too-close houses,
protest the proposed, too-close store
and the too many new neighbors—
as if the issues are more simple
than when neighbors protested and detested you.
You say you want to simplify,
yet you say it looking to the floor—
as if nobody here is in charge.

Draft 2

You say you want to simplify,
and you will—
someday soon.
But, today,

there is so much money
and so little time to build
what everyone wants,
what the marketplace demands.
(Damn those who would protest and detest!)
Today there are the kids to get through college,
the liability insurance,
and the mortgage on the new house
with the giant kitchen that you hope to use
during the more simple times ahead.
Every day you say,
"This rat race must end someday."
You say you want to simplify.
You say it through a portable telephone,
yet you say it looking to the sky—
as if nobody here is in charge.

Draft 3

You say you want to simplify,
to ecologize,
yet you drive this off-road,
four-wheel-drive,

chrome beauty
that guzzles and spews all over town
and never leaves the highway—
but leaves you with the option and the image.
This beauty might help you through a snowstorm
when you might better stay at home—
stay off the road,
act humbly before your mother nature
who says,
"A better off-road vehicle
 would encourage you to keep off the roads."
Oh, but yours is pretty,
has status,
and looks "back-to-the-earth".
You say you want to ecologize,
yet your trusted, rusted truck takes you
to where you want to be,
to what you want to be,
when you want to show
at the rally to protect the river
and keep the rascal developer
from building more houses like your own—
houses for new romantic ecologizers

with more off-road,
four-wheel-drive,
chrome beauties,
streamlined coaches,
and trusted, rusted trucks.
More new neighbors,
(kindred spirits)
who pursue your dream
and wonder why
(as hard as they try)
they too don't catch it.

Draft 4

You say you want to simplify,
yet you send your kid to private school,
(a damn good school)
quite expensive enough
to make you earn more money
and need a better, bigger, streamlined coach
to drive him
(and his friends of yours)
back and forth,

and then to soccer practice
and music lessons.
Yet you wonder why
life does not simplify.
Your kid is at fault.
Thank god you don't have four or five!
How did they manage in the olden days
(a few decades ago)
when you were a kid
and life was more simple,
and you walked,
took a bus,
rode your bike
without a loving, nagging parent at your side
(always there for you)
when you are needed.
It must have been a miracle back then.
But your mom did nothing important,
and your dad was nobody important,
and your house was no place special—
except maybe home.
But even the hard life seemed more simple,
and none among you was perfect.

It is so damn complex
to make life perfect these days,
if not for you,
(no, yes, yes perfect for you, but especially)
for your kid who will be forever indebted
for all you have done for him:
sacrifice,
stress,
unhappiness
so he could have a simple life—
and, perhaps, recognize it.
An example would be nice.
Freedom too would be nice for him,
to be imperfect,
to get lost,
to fool around,
to get around on his two feet,
on the public street,
that public school
of complex evolution,
sticks and stones,
strange tones,
the place where adults and children develop.

Draft 5

You say you want to simplify,
yet you dry your just-wet hair
with a hot, electric blower.
And you want to remove
(for a moment)
the leaves from your walk
with a cold, electric blower.
Don't you know,
real men don't blow their hair dry,
and real women aren't supposed to be sissies.
At least, they weren't and didn't
when man and woman were "boy and girl",
and they looked sexy in damp hair
and looked romantic on leaf-covered walks.
So, you say you want to simplify,
then call the Center For Disease Control
to find out who ever died,
(or even caught a sniffle)
from stepping out
in the cool of autumn
under damp hair,
or, for that matter,

under wet hair
in the dead of winter.
So, conduct a sweepers-and-blowers race
on your local sidewalk.
Watch the blowers come in third
and the sweepers come in second
to the walking, damp-haired cruncher
who passes them by—
enjoying the comic scene
while enjoying the simple crunch
of leaves under her feet.
Then ask the damp-haired cruncher
to open and show them the one-small bag
she packs along on her extended travels.
Then hear them whisper:
"There must be a trick.
 She is secretly rich—has a rich lover.
 How else could she make it look so simple?"

Draft 6

You say you want to simplify,
purify and purge,

yet you park your combusting motor
twenty-nine feet from your exercise club,
your health club—
what a body!
All those bodies covered with sweat!
How many dollars per drop?
How much asphalt to park the car bodies,
trucks,
fetishes?
How much energy to air condition your arrival?
Because it would be too simple
to sweat your way there,
walk there,
run there,
ride there on your beautiful muscle power.
So, you want to simplify,
then hang a sign on your clubhouse door:
"!If You Drove Here You Do Not Belong!"
Do that, and it won't be long
before people blush
as they walk in from the parking lot,
(chins down)
sneak in,

apologize.
It won't be much longer
before they walk in
(chins up)
from their houses,
from their offices,
from their playgrounds
a couple of miles away.
And not much longer
until they get together to proclaim:
"City Law Forbids Motor Parking
  With Intent To Enter A Health Club."
Now, you have started a revolution:
healthy clubs,
healthy people,
simple people,
and a few public showers,
(and private showers)
and climbing towers
simply placed
along the ways where we like to sweat.

Final Draft

You say you want to simplify,
purify and purge,
ecologize,
survive.
Life is too hectic.
You yearn for less.
OK.
Look ahead!
Good luck!
Send a postcard!
You are in charge.

Victory

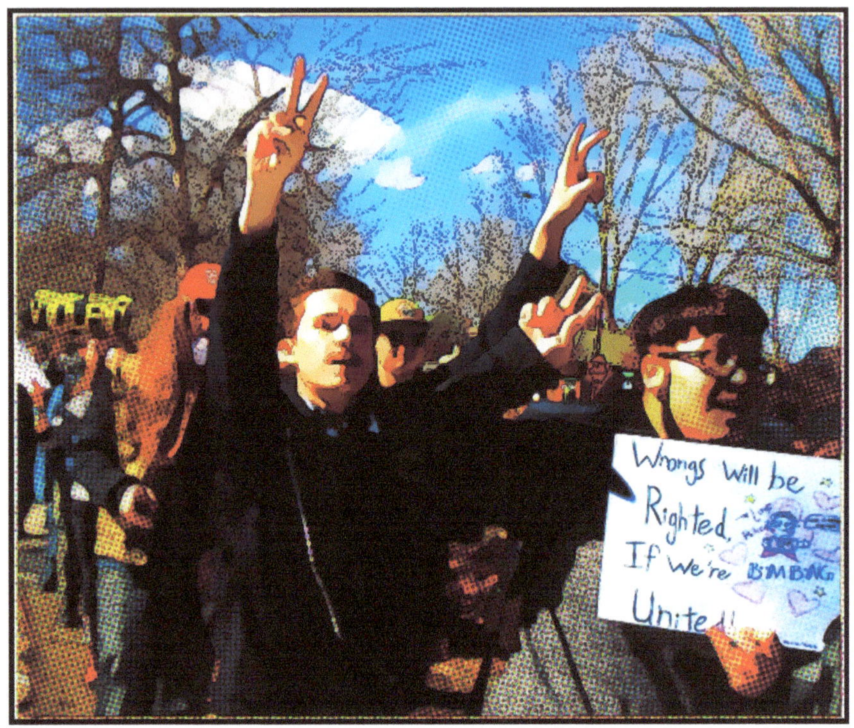

With early victory come sunbeams.
Later, come smoke and ash that hide defeat.

We now retreat,
but first we won
over.whelm.ing.ly.

We thought we knew
to administer our place,
to celebrate our art,
to hand our wisdom
to generations that we would save from history.
Soon, we end retreat,
regroup and wait,
to remember how victory came
and forget which way it went.
So, let us post now an order to govern our attack
when we take back the larger part.
Some of us
(duty bound)
must turn coat
to defend retreating enemy
and there defend our victory.

Early victory brings sunbeams.
Total victory portends defeat.
Let us stop this time where the sun shines.

Love And Passion

Dear Love And Passion
I mourn the fashion
when you were the rage.
You said, “love our neighbors;
You said, “make love;
You said, “don't make war.”
You said we were tied in knots, up-tight, inside and out, unable to know what it's like to be human.
You wanted the best for us all,
—work and play for the best—
and if we got less,
if we got the worst,
then, with passion
and with love,
let's mourn and celebrate our mourning,
for that too is to be human.
Yes, there were arrogance and excess;
we made an occasional mess when you were the rage.

Some people wanted to be loved without loving,
to make love without giving.

Others conveniently forgot about peace.
But I think I remember that your message was clear:
"accept ourselves;
"accept each other;
"work and play for a dream that includes us all;
"do these with love and with passion."
Amidst all those -isms that brought us so much lying and killing
you refused to imprison your message in a dogma.

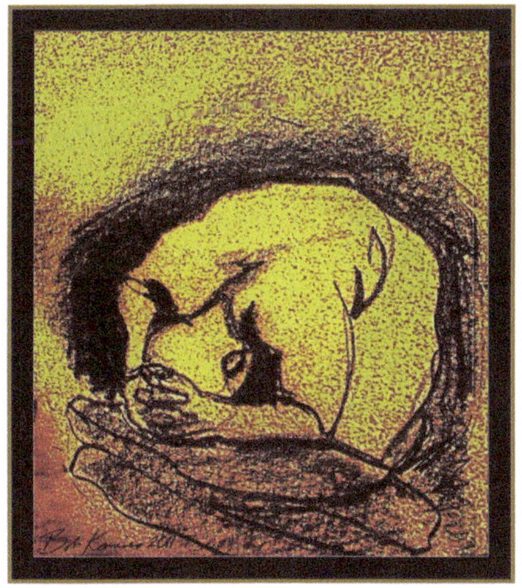

Yet, you encouraged those who pursued other -isms,
one, erotic but loving,
one, passive but passionate,
one, simply human.

Now, is it an eon or an age
since you were the rage
and you held your head up high?
For so long it has been so different.
Today, for your universal love we get a kind of family in a fuzzy painting that maybe we could see better if we wore the right prescription over our eyes.
For your acceptance of amorous passion we get a passion for hate —a passion that would dispense with those who are different and with those who just disagree.
But, they, whom we hate, hate us equally.
We hate them for that.
For your fun and your play we get games of deadly embrace in which hated and hated try to win one before supper.
For your sharing of need and plenty we get greed for what we want. For what we want is what we need, and what we need we may get, and what we get makes us better.
If we do not try to get we have a defect in character.

Your innocent way gets all the blame for today,
in case you haven't heard.

We must now deal with a real disease that can kill us
for making love.
You taught us to think of mutual pleasure.
Now, we think of our personal safety.
Pleasure and joy are slightly out of fashion.
Sex is still in.
It gives us topics and teases for sales and for politics,
but it is bad again.
If we cannot be alone, then, for god's sake, let's marry and have but one partner and then pray that one of us does not twist our love into abuse.
If we happen to find our neighbor abused or otherwise bleeding, then, for safety's sake, for blame's sake, stand back; call an ambulance.
This does not feel right.
You said,
"it is right only if it feels right," but to quote you today is a crime.
Now, we say:
"if it feels wrong it may still be legal; they probably won't sue us anyway; and we can find a verse assigned to god that says it's right."
How has this happened?
We hear that you are to blame for it all.

Are you?

Your official name is now Lust And Desire.

Most folks just call you Irresponsible.

Are you to blame?

I hope not.

You were so positive.

You liked us.

You liked our possibilities.

You left suburbia to move into the city and out to the country where we noticed each other.

No one seems to notice us anymore.

No one seems to like us anymore.

A few of us like some of us, but you were the last one to like us all.

None of us seems to like where we are going, but we are all sure that another automobile and a bigger refrigerator will make our journey nicer.

Our children are now our passengers.

We take them everywhere they have to go,

but we doubt that they will be glad they went.

Do you remember when we went about chanting,

"there is no free lunch!"?

Well, everyone remembers those words,

yet few seem to understand what they mean.

I remember a chant:
"liberty, life, pursuit of happiness!"
I think you called them free love,
but my memory is vague.
I don't remember that I defended you.
There were so many others
who defended you so well.
Now, if I were to try,
I am not sure anyone would listen—many, because they despise
you, most, because they have forgotten.
I remember—just enough.
I remember your visit just enough to want another.

I hope sincerely, dear Love And Passion,
that if perhaps you can return to fashion
you come within my dwindling stock of more days.

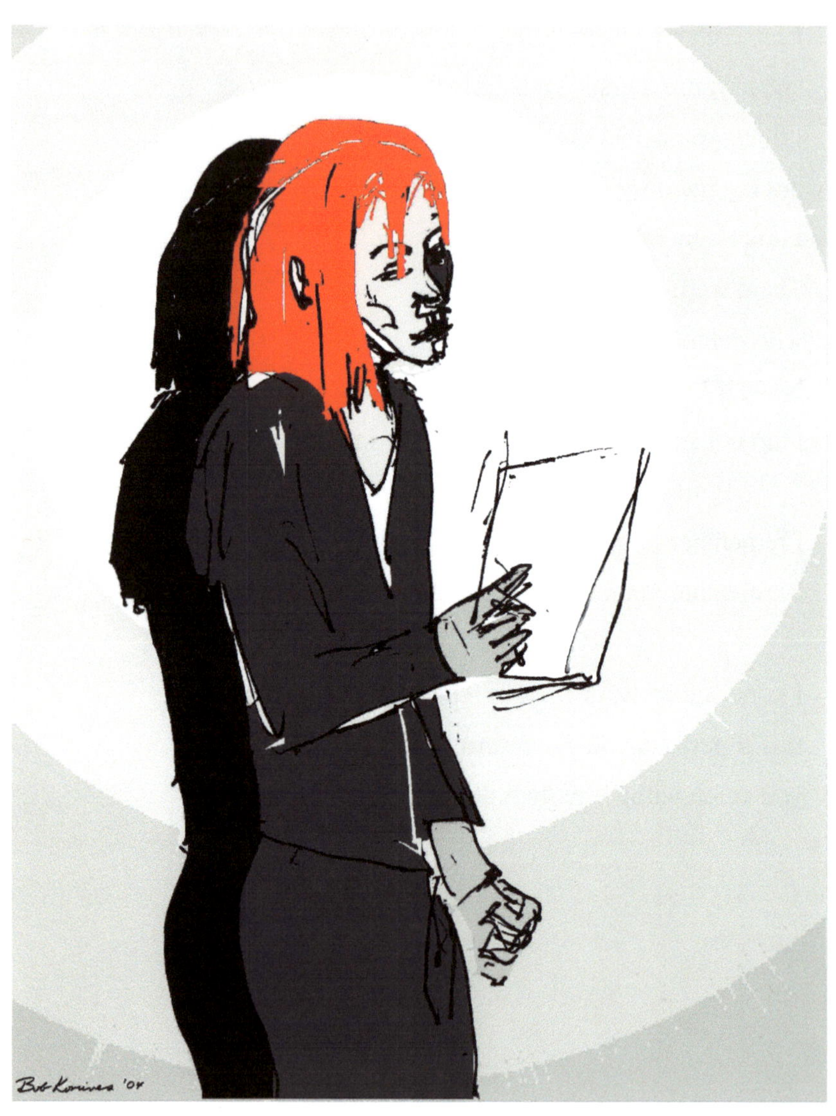

I Speak of Memory

I speak of memory,
to retell from memory
a story that has waited long for recall.

You did not request this recall
nor offer your approval.
Nor do I seek approval,
nor make claim of perfect recollection,
nor accuse yours of imperfection.

I retell this story
because I want not to forget,
and because I hope you want to remember.
I know I tell no lie
and make no intentional distortion,
wishing it unnecessary to say so.
As to certainty,
when with it, I strive to be humble;
when without it, I strive to be honest.

Will my retelling be, in places, mistaken?
Likely, yes.

Will I do harm with my truth
or my mistake?
Likely, no,
but I admit the risk.

From past retellings
I know that memory does play tricks
but plays no less with you than with me.
And silence
is this trickster's favorite play yard.
I hope recollective voice
helps collective memory
among us who lived that time.

For you may wish to answer the curious
who were not there then,
or educate the ignorant
who do not care now.

You may wish to speak out from our memory
or you may prefer to live more fully
within in the fullness of secrets we share.

And so I begin.

And so I end.

I have retold our story.
You have listened.
If you do not remember as I,
I hope you will remember why I speak.

---

the end